# Reading/Writing Companion

Mc
Graw
Hill

mheducation.com/prek-12

Copyright © 2023 McGraw Hill

All rights reserved. No part of this publication may be
reproduced or distributed in any form or by any means,
or stored in a database or retrieval system, without the
prior written consent of McGraw Hill, including, but not
limited to, network storage or transmission, or broadcast
for distance learning.

Send all inquiries to:
McGraw Hill
1325 Avenue of the Americas
New York, NY 10019

ISBN: 978-1-26-576121-9
MHID: 1-26-576121-3

Printed in the United States of America.

5 6 7 8 9 LMN 26 25 24 23 22            B

# Welcome to WONDERS!

We're here to help you set goals to build on the amazing things you already know. We'll also help you reflect on everything you'll learn.

Let's start by taking a look at the incredible things you'll do this year.

You'll build knowledge on exciting topics and find answers to interesting questions.

You'll read fascinating fiction, informational texts, and poetry and respond to what you read with your own thoughts and ideas.

And you'll research and write stories, poems, and essays of your own!

Here's a sneak peek at how you'll do it all.

## *"Let's go!"*

You'll explore new ideas by reading groups of different texts about the same topic. These groups of texts are called *text sets*.

At the beginning of a text set, we'll help you set goals on the My Goals page. You'll see a bar with four boxes beneath each goal. Think about what you already know to fill in the bar. Here's an example.

**I can read and understand expository text.**

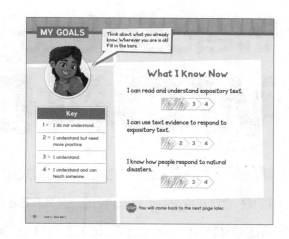

As you move through a text set, you'll explore an essential question and build your knowledge of a topic until you're ready to write about it yourself.

You'll also learn skills that will help you reach your text set goals. At the end of lessons, you'll see a new Check In bar with four boxes.

CHECK IN   1   2   3   4

Reflect on how well you understood a lesson to fill in the bar.

**Here are some questions you can ask yourself.**

- Was I able to complete the task?

- Was it easy, or was it hard?

- Do I think I need more practice?

At the end of each text set, you'll show off the knowledge you built by completing a fun task. Then you'll return to the second My Goals page where we'll help you reflect on all that you learned.

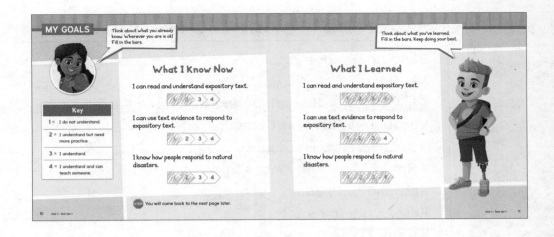

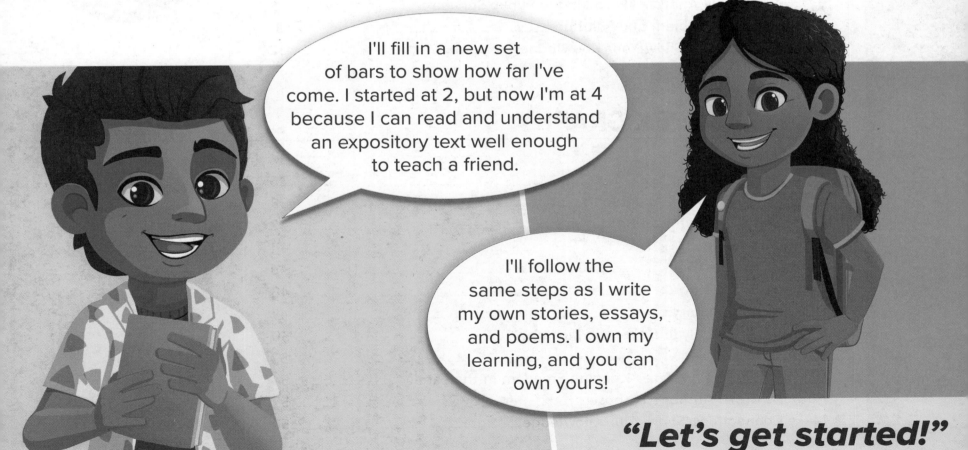

*"Let's get started!"*

# TEXT SET 1 **REALISTIC FICTION**

# TEXT SET 2 **BIOGRAPHY**

# TEXT SET 3 **ARGUMENTATIVE TEXT**

# EXTENDED WRITING

# CONNECT AND REFLECT

**Digital Tools**

Find this eBook and
other resources at
**my.mheducation.com**

John Lamb/The Image Bank/Getty Images

# TEXT SET 1 **NARRATIVE NONFICTION**

# TEXT SET 2 **HISTORICAL FICTION**

# TEXT SET 3 **NARRATIVE POETRY**

# EXTENDED WRITING

# CONNECT AND REFLECT

**Digital Tools**
Find this eBook and
other resources at
**my.mheducation.com**

Tony Anderson/The Image Bank/Getty Images

# Build Knowledge

# Build Vocabulary

Write new words you learned about how people can help their community. Draw lines and circles for the words you write.

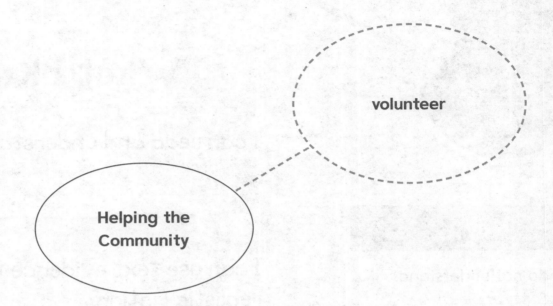

volunteer

Helping the Community

Go online to **my.mheducation.com** and read the "Let's Pitch In!" Blast. Why do you think it's important that people help out in their community? Blast back your response.

Think about what you already know. Fill in the bars. This will be a good start.

## What I Know Now

I can read and understand realistic fiction.

| 1 | 2 | 3 | 4 |

I can use text evidence to respond to realistic fiction.

| 1 | 2 | 3 | 4 |

I know ways I can help my community.

| 1 | 2 | 3 | 4 |

**Key**

**1** = I do not understand.

**2** = I understand but need more practice.

**3** = I understand.

**4** = I understand and can teach someone.

**STOP** You will come back to the next page later.

Think about what you learned.
Fill in the bars. What are you getting better at?

# What I Learned

I can read and understand realistic fiction.

| 1 | 2 | 3 | 4 |

I can use text evidence to respond to realistic fiction.

| 1 | 2 | 3 | 4 |

I know ways I can help my community.

| 1 | 2 | 3 | 4 |

**My Goal** I can read and understand realistic fiction.

### TAKE NOTES

As you read, make note of interesting words and important details.

# REMEMBERING HURRICANE KATRINA

### Essential Question

**?** In what ways can you help your community?

Read about how Hector helps others after Hurricane Katrina.

Thomas Barwick/Photodisc/Getty Images; Blend Images/SuperStock; Tyrone Turner/National Geographic/Getty Images; all other images by Jeff Mangiat

Leaning over my steering wheel, I watched the heavy clouds roll in. The sky became a darker shade of gray, and raindrops were soon **scattered** across my windshield. A storm was coming. Glancing at the boxes of clothes stacked in the backseat, I smiled to myself.

A torrential downpour of rain began beating against my windshield as lightning flickered across the sky. I pulled the car off the road until my driving visibility improved. People on the sidewalk held purses and briefcases over their heads in a futile effort to keep from getting wet. Children screamed and danced around in the downpour. The rain reminded me of another storm ten years earlier.

Hurricane Katrina slammed into the Gulf Coast of the United States when I was nine years old. The ferocious storm caused untold amounts of damage.

One of my strongest memories from that time was watching the evening news with my aunt. A reporter stood inside the Houston Astrodome, surrounded by thousands of people. They all shared the same weary expression. Many wore torn and dirty clothes, and some had no shoes on their feet. They slowly shuffled along, their faces full of sadness.

Jeff Mangiat

## FIND TEXT EVIDENCE

**Read**

Paragraphs 1–2

### Narrator's Point of View

**Draw a box** around the pronouns that show that the narrator is a character in the story.

### Character Perspective

**Underline** the sentence in paragraph 2 that tells you Hector is thinking about an event that happened in the past. What is the event?

_____

_____

Paragraphs 3–4

### Visualize

**Circle** the words in paragraph 4 that help you picture in your mind the people inside the Astrodome.

**Reread**

### Author's Craft

How does the author show the impact Hurricane Katrina had on Hector?

### FIND TEXT EVIDENCE

**Read**

Paragraphs 1–3

**Narrator's Point of View**

**Draw a box** around the sentence that tells you Hector is the narrator.

**Character Perspective**

**Underline** the details in paragraph 3 that tell why Hector is worried that Hurricane Katrina might be a problem for his community.

Paragraphs 4–6
**Context Clues**

**Circle** the context clue in paragraph 5 that helps you figure out the meaning of *devised*. Write the meaning below.

_____

_____

**Reread**

**Author's Craft**

What can you tell about Hector by the way he acted during Hurricane Katrina?

"Are they here because of the hurricane?" I asked softly.

Aunt Lucia nodded. "*Sí*, Hector. These people are from New Orleans, Louisiana. Just a few days ago, Hurricane Katrina destroyed their homes and possessions, and they lost everything they owned, so now they are temporary **residents** of the Astrodome. It's a place for them to stay until it's safe to go home."

I knew a lot about Katrina. The storm had formed in hot and humid tropical weather and then traveled north. It had come so close to Texas that I worried it would strike us in Houston. It missed us, but other cities were not so lucky.

The TV news reporter looked around. People tried to speak to her, but she was being **selective** about whom she wanted to interview. I noticed a little boy sitting behind her on a cot, hugging an old teddy bear. Watching him, I knew I had to do something.

The next day, my friends joined me at our volunteer club—the Houston Helpers—and together we devised a plan. We wanted to collect toys and give them to the kids at the Astrodome because donating the toys would help bring some happiness into the lives of these families.

Anxious to get started, we made lists of what we needed to do. Then every one of us was **assigned** a specific task.

We agreed to spread the word to our schools and other **organizations**. Three days later, after a Herculean effort on our part, the donation bins were overflowing with new toys!

I'll never forget the day when we entered the Astrodome with our gifts. Children flew toward us from all directions. Smiles lit up their faces as we pulled toys from our bags. Grateful parents thanked us for our **generosity** and complimented our group leaders on how thoughtful and **mature** we all were.

*BZZZZ.* My cell phone jolted me back to the present, and I noticed that the storm had passed.

"Hector?"

"*Sí*, yes, hi, Jeannie."

"Do you have the donations? A few more families have arrived, more victims of yesterday's tornado."

"Yes, I have the clothing donations. The storm delayed me, but I'll be there soon!"

I **gingerly** eased my car into the suddenly busy traffic. It felt good to know that I was making a difference again.

Jeffrey Mangiat

## Summarize

Use your notes to summarize the plot and theme of "Remembering Hurricane Katrina."

## REALISTIC FICTION

### FIND TEXT EVIDENCE

**Read**

Paragraphs 1–2

**Visualize**

**Circle** the details in paragraph 2 that help you visualize the reactions of the people in the Astrodome.

Paragraphs 3–8

**Plot: Flashback**

What event happens that brings the story back to the present?

_____

_____

_____

**Reread**

**Author's Craft**

How did Hurricane Katrina influence what Hector is doing today?

# Vocabulary

**Use the example sentences to talk with a partner about each word. Then answer the questions.**

### assigned

The teacher **assigned** the class a book report for next week.

What has a teacher assigned your class recently?

_____

_____

### generosity

The children show their **generosity** by collecting food for people in need.

What are some words associated with generosity?

_____

_____

### gingerly

I stepped **gingerly** into the cold water of the lake.

What is a reason you might step gingerly?

_____

_____

### mature

Mom says I am **mature** enough to babysit my little sister.

What is an antonym for _mature_?

_____

_____

### organizations

There are many different **organizations** that help people in need.

What are some organizations that help people in your town or city?

_____

_____

 **Build Your Word List** Pick one of the interesting words you noted on page 12 and look up its meaning in a print or online dictionary. In your reader's notebook, write two sentences using that word: a statement and a question.

**residents**

The **residents** of our neighborhood had a food drive.

What activities do the residents of your town or city do?

_____

_____

**scattered**

The papers were **scattered** all over the floor.

What is a synonym for *scattered*?

_____

_____

**selective**

My father makes healthful meals, so he is **selective** about the food he buys.

What are you selective about?

_____

_____

## Context Clues

As you read "Remembering Hurricane Katrina," you may come across a word you don't know. A definition of the word may be in the text nearby, or the word may be restated in a simpler way.

### 🔍 FIND TEXT EVIDENCE

*When I read the fifth paragraph on page 14, the phrase* collect toys and give them *helps me figure out what the word* donating *means.*

We wanted to  to the kids at the Astrodome because donating the toys would help bring some happiness into the lives of these families.

**Your Turn** Use context clues to figure out the meanings of the following words.

**shuffled**, page 13 _____

_____

**possessions**, page 14 _____

_____

CHECK IN ⟩ 1 ⟩ 2 ⟩ 3 ⟩ 4 ⟩

# Visualize

When you read fiction, try to visualize, or picture, the events, characters, and setting in your mind. This will better help you understand the characters' experiences and what happens in the story.

## 🔍 FIND TEXT EVIDENCE

*On page 13 of "Remembering Hurricane Katrina," I can use the details to picture the setting. The narrator describes the rain, the lightning, and the people on the sidewalk holding briefcases and purses over their heads.*

Page 13

> Leaning over my steering wheel, I watched the heavy clouds roll in. The sky became a darker shade of gray, and raindrops were soon **scattered** across my windshield. A storm was coming. . . .
>
> A torrential downpour of rain began beating against my windshield as lightning flickered across the sky. I pulled the car off the road until my driving visibility improved. People on the sidewalk held purses and briefcases over their heads in a futile effort to keep from getting wet. Children screamed and danced around in the downpour.

*The author describes the sky, the changing weather, and people's actions. I can use these descriptive details to visualize what the setting looks and sounds like. This helps me better understand what Hector is experiencing.*

**Your Turn** Visualize the scene between Hector and his aunt as they watch the news report. Describe what you "see" to a partner. Remember to use the Visualize strategy.

---

**Quick Tip**

As you read, look for sensory words that describe sight, sound, smell, taste, and touch. Phrases like *lightning flickered* and *rain began beating against my windshield* help the reader to visualize the storm.

---

CHECK IN  1  2  3  4

# Plot: Flashback

"Remembering Hurricane Katrina" is realistic fiction. Realistic fiction is a made-up story with realistic characters, dialogue, events, and settings. The plot may include a flashback to an earlier event. Being able to identify flashbacks will help you understand the time order of events and how these events affect the plot.

 **FIND TEXT EVIDENCE**

*I can tell "Remembering Hurricane Katrina" is realistic fiction. The characters, dialogue, events, and setting could all exist in real life. In the flashback, we learn how an earlier storm affected Hector.*

### Readers to Writers

Writers use flashbacks to help readers better understand a character or situation. By explaining what happened in the past, readers know why characters feel or act the way they do in the present. How characters act and feel in response to events shows the characters' development. How can you use flashbacks in your own writing?

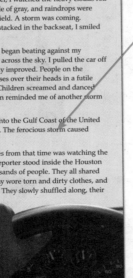

Page 13

Leaning over my steering wheel, I watched the heavy clouds roll in. The sky became a darker shade of gray, and raindrops were soon **scattered** across my windshield. A storm was coming. Glancing at the boxes of clothes stacked in the backseat, I smiled to myself.

A torrential downpour of rain began beating against my windshield as lightning flickered across the sky. I pulled the car off the road until my driving visibility improved. People on the sidewalk held purses and briefcases over their heads in a futile effort to keep from getting wet. Children screamed and danced around in the downpour. The rain reminded me of another storm ten years earlier.

Hurricane Katrina slammed into the Gulf Coast of the United States when I was nine years old. The ferocious storm caused untold amounts of damage.

One of my strongest memories from that time was watching the evening news with my aunt. A reporter stood inside the Houston Astrodome, surrounded by thousands of people. They all shared the same weary expression. Many wore torn and dirty clothes, and some had no shoes on their feet. They slowly shuffled along, their faces full of sadness.

### Flashback

Sometimes authors do not present a story's events in time order. Authors might take the reader back to an event that happened in the past. This is called a *flashback*.

 **Your Turn** What do the events in the flashback help you understand about Hector? How do these events affect the plot?

COLLABORATE

_____

_____

_____

_____

CHECK IN ⟩ 1 ⟩ 2 ⟩ 3 ⟩ 4 ⟩

# Point of View and Perspective

*Narrator's point of view* refers to the type of narrator, or storyteller, telling the story. A first-person narrator is a character in the story. The narrator uses the pronouns *I, me, my, we, our,* and *us.*

*Character perspective* refers to how a character thinks or feels about something or someone.

## 🔍 FIND TEXT EVIDENCE

*On page 13 of "Remembering Hurricane Katrina," the narrator uses the pronouns* I, me, *and* my. *That tells me the story is told by a first-person narrator. Hector is the narrator. I can find clues in the text about Hector's perspective.*

| Details |
|---|
| Hector remembers watching the hurricane victims slowly shuffling along with faces full of sadness. |
| Hector noticed a little boy hugging an old teddy bear and realized he had to do something. |

↓

| Character Perspective |
|---|
| Hector thinks it is important to help the hurricane victims. |

Jeffrey Mangiat

**Your Turn** Reread "Remembering Hurricane Katrina." Find other details that tell Hector's perspective. List them in the graphic organizer on page 21.

> **Quick Tip**
>
> - In **first-person point of view**, the narrator is a character in the story. All the events are seen through the eyes of that character.
>
> - In **third-person point of view**, the narrator is not in the story. The narrator tells about the characters' perspectives using pronouns such as *he, she, they, his, her, their,* and *them.*

**CHECK IN** 1 > 2 > 3 > 4

| Details |
|---|
| |
| |
| |

| Character Perspective |
|---|
| |

# Respond to Reading

Discuss the prompt below. Use your notes and text evidence to support your response.

How did Hurricane Katrina affect Hector? What can readers learn from this?

_____

_____

_____

_____

_____

_____

_____

_____

_____

_____

_____

_____

_____

_____

## Quick Tip

Use these sentence starters to discuss the text and organize your ideas.

- *Hector thinks back to the days following Hurricane Katrina because . . .*
- *Hector decides to help by . . .*
- *From Hector's actions, readers can learn that . . .*

## Grammar Connections

As you write your response, check your use of possessive nouns. For plural nouns that end in -s, add only the apostrophe to the end of the noun: *the friends' donations.*

**CHECK IN** 1 2 3 4

# Volunteering in Your Community

Volunteering is a great way to help your community. Follow the research process to create a radio public service announcement (PSA) that promotes a volunteering opportunity in your community. Work with a partner.

**Step 1**   **Set a Goal** Generate questions you want your research about volunteer opportunities to answer.

**Step 2**   **Identify Sources** Use newspapers, websites, and talking to people you know to find information about local volunteer opportunities. Choose one of the volunteer opportunities to focus on.

**Step 3**   **Find and Record Information** Take notes that tell about the responsibilities and other key details of the position. Try to answer the questions you came up with in the beginning of the research process.

**Step 4**   **Organize and Synthesize Information** Organize your notes. Include information about the requirements and responsibilities of the volunteering position and why it is important to the community.

**Step 5**   **Create and Present** Write the script for your PSA. After you finish, think about how you will present it to your class.

### Quick Tip

When searching for information on the Internet, type keywords, or words that are most related to the subject, into the search engine. Typing keywords, such as *volunteer* and the name of your community, into a search engine will help you find websites that will tell you about volunteering locally.

**CHECK IN** 〉 1 〉 2 〉 3 〉 4

# Aguinaldo

Literature Anthology:
pages 178–189

**?** **How do you know how Marilia feels about going on the field trip?**

**Talk About It** Reread paragraphs 1–4 on **Literature Anthology** page 183. Turn to your partner and talk about the last thing Marilia has to do.

**Cite Text Evidence** What clues help you understand what Marilia was feeling about going on the field trip? Write evidence and what it means in the chart.

### Make Inferences

When you read about Marilia's actions, what inference can you make about how Marilia will deal with problems she has in the future?

| Clue |
|---|

↓

| Clue |
|---|

↓

| Clue |
|---|

↓

| How Marilia Feels |
|---|

**Write** I know how Marilia feels about going on the field trip because the author _____

_____

CHECK IN 1 2 3 4

**How does the author use dialogue to show the relationship between Elenita and Marilia?**

**Talk About It** Reread the first four paragraphs on **Literature Anthology** page 187. Turn to your partner and discuss what Elenita and Marilia talk about.

**Cite Text Evidence** What clues help you figure out how they are getting along? Write text evidence in the chart.

| Clues | Elenita and Marilia |
|-------|---------------------|
|       |                     |

**Write** The author uses dialogue to show that Elenita and Marilia are

_____

_____

**Quick Tip**

Work with a partner. Discuss how the characters would sound if they were talking to each other. Would they speak loudly or quietly, in a friendly or unfriendly tone? Act out the dialogue in the first four paragraphs on page 187. As you read the dialogue, use gestures and facial expressions.

Use these sentence starters to discuss the dialogue.

- *The dialogue between two characters helps the reader understand . . .*
- *I think Elenita and Marilia will . . .*

CHECK IN  1  2  3  4

? How does what Marilia tells Margarita on the bus trip back to school help you understand how Marilia feels?

COLLABORATE

**Talk About It** Reread the last three paragraphs on **Literature Anthology** page 188. Turn to your partner and discuss what Margarita and Marilia talk about on the bus.

**Cite Text Evidence** What does Marilia say that shows how she feels? Write text evidence in the chart.

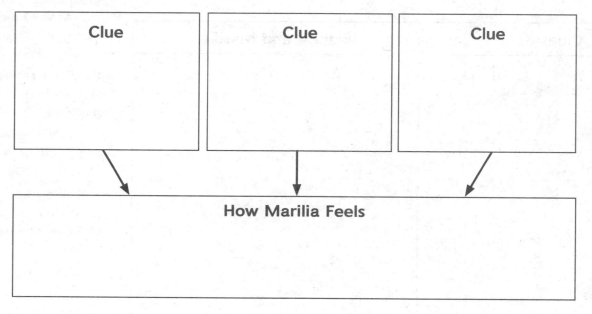

| Clue | Clue | Clue |
|------|------|------|
|      |      |      |

**How Marilia Feels**

**Write** The author uses Margarita and Marilia's conversation to help show that _____

_____

_____

_____

**Quick Tip**

When you reread, you can use what the characters say to understand their feelings and actions.

Use these sentence starters to describe the characters.

- *Marilia cares about Elenita because . . .*
- *Elenita probably feels that Marilia is . . .*

**Synthesize Information**

Combine what you have learned about Marilia from the beginning of the story to the end of the story. What did Marilia learn from her visit to the nursing home? How do you know she learned this?

**CHECK IN** 1 2 3 4

# Respond to Reading

Discuss the prompt below. Use your notes and text evidence to support your response.

How does the class field trip to the nursing home affect Marilia? Why do Marilia's feelings about the nursing home change from the beginning of the story to the end?

_____

_____

_____

_____

_____

_____

_____

_____

_____

_____

_____

_____

_____

**Quick Tip**

Use these sentence starters to discuss the prompt and to organize your ideas.

- *Marilia doesn't want to go to the nursing home because . . .*

- *Marilia eventually approaches Elenita because . . .*

- *Marilia says she likes Elenita after . . .*

CHECK IN  1  2  3  4

# Partaking in Public Service

Literature Anthology:
pages 192–195

### There is no doubt about it:

[1]    Volunteering is an important part of American life. About 27% of us volunteer in some way. This means that one American out of every four is performing a public service. Many volunteers are teens and children. In fact, in the last 20 years, the number of teen volunteers in this country has doubled. Youth service organizations, such as 4-H clubs, have grown in popularity.

[2]    Kids join local volunteer groups to give back to their communities. They work together to help others and to improve their schools and neighborhoods. Community projects may include planting gardens or collecting food and clothing. Some kids raise money for local charities. The volunteer opportunities are limitless.

Reread paragraph 1. **Underline** the clue that tells how the author feels about volunteering. **Circle** two examples in the paragraph that support the author's statement.

Reread paragraph 2 and look at the bar graph. Talk with a partner about how the bar graph helps you understand how kids volunteer.

In the bar graph, **circle** the top volunteer activity for kids. **Draw a box** around the activity that about 21 percent of kids volunteer to do.

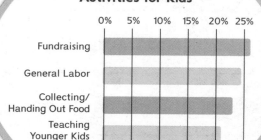

**Top Four Volunteer Activities for Kids**

0% 5% 10% 15% 20% 25%

Fundraising

General Labor

Collecting/ Handing Out Food

Teaching Younger Kids

1    Alex Lin was just nine years old when he formed the WIN community service team to recycle electronics. By the time he was 16, he had recycled 300,000 pounds of e-waste. He also helped to write a law against e-waste in his home state of Rhode Island.

2    Alex soon realized that reusing was an even better solution to e-waste. Working with his school, he set up a program that fixed old computers and donated them to students in need. Eventually, this program grew. Now it sends computers to people around the world.

3    Erica Fernandez also cares about the environment. She was 16 years old when she heard that a natural gas plant would be built near her hometown. Erica learned that the plant would pollute the air. It would bring harmful chemicals to nearby towns.

4    Erica decided to do something about it. She organized groups to protest the plant. They spoke out publicly. They wrote letters to the government. Eventually, the state agreed to cancel the plans for the plant. Thanks to Erica, the local environment was saved.

Reread paragraphs 1 to 4. **Underline** text evidence in paragraph 1 that tells what Alex recycles. **Circle** evidence in paragraph 1 that tells how he helped Rhode Island. Then **draw a box** around text evidence in paragraph 2 that tells why he started fixing old computers.

Talk with a partner about how Alex's and Erica's projects are both alike and different. **Put checkmarks** in the margin beside the similarities between Alex and Erica and their projects. Write the similarities here.

_____

_____

_____

_____

_____

_____

**?** How does the author use what other young people have done to help you see how you can make a difference?

**Talk About It** Reread paragraphs 1 to 4 on page 29. Talk with a partner about how kids can volunteer.

**Cite Text Evidence** How does the author help you see that you can make a difference, too? Write text evidence in the chart.

| What Alex Did | What Erica Did | I See That |
| --- | --- | --- |
| | | |

**Write** The author uses real-life examples of young people who volunteer

to _____

_____

_____

_____

**Quick Tip**

The author tells about young people who thought of ways to help make a difference in the world.

With a partner, think about something that would help make the world a better place.

Use these sentence starters.

- *I think it would be a good idea . . .*
- *This idea could help make the world a better place because . . .*

CHECK IN  1  2  3  4

# Problem and Solution

An author decides how to present, or organize, information in a text. One type of text structure that authors use is **problem and solution.** In a problem-and-solution text structure, the author presents a problem and then tells the solution, or the steps taken to solve the problem.

 **FIND TEXT EVIDENCE**

In paragraph 3 on page 29 of "Partaking in Public Service," the author tells a problem: "Erica learned that the plant would pollute the air." In the next paragraph, the first sentence alerts the reader that Erica is going to try to find a solution: "Erica decided to do something about it." The rest of the paragraph tells about her solution.

> Erica decided to do something about it. She organized groups to protest the plant. They spoke out publicly. They wrote letters to the government. Eventually, the state agreed to cancel the plans for the plant.

**Your Turn** Reread paragraphs 2, 3, and 4 on page 194 in the **Literature Anthology.**

- What problem is the author telling about? _____

_____

- What steps does Alex take to solve the problem? _____

_____

_____

CHECK IN  1  2  3  4

---

**Readers to Writers**

When you are writing information, think about what text structure will best help your audience understand the information. You can have the same text structure for your whole essay, or you can have different text structures for different paragraphs. Choose what works best for your purpose.

Text structures include

- *problem and solution*
- *chronology*
- *comparison*
- *cause and effect*
- *sequence*
- *description*

# MAKE CONNECTIONS

**?** **What ideas about community are shown by the illustration on this page? How are these ideas similar to the idea of community in *Aguinaldo* and "Partaking in Public Service"?**

**Talk About It** Look at the illustration and read the caption. Talk about what you see happening. Discuss how charity events help the community.

**Cite Text Evidence** **Underline** the people in the illustration who are helping other people. **Circle** the images that tell you where the walk is taking place. Think about how the characters in *Aguinaldo* and the kids in "Partaking in Public Service" help you understand the meaning of community.

**Write** The ideas about community in the illustration are similar to the ideas in *Aguinaldo* and "Partaking in Public Service" because _____

_____

_____

_____

_____

_____

**Quick Tip**

Look at the illustration and discuss how people are participating in a community event.

*People are participating in a charity event by . . .*

*People are helping each other by . . .*

Twelve community members participating in a charity event in their local park

ImageZoo/SuperStock

**CHECK IN** 1 2 3 4

## Write a Song

Think about what you learned about people helping in their communities. What are some things that motivate people to help out?

1. Look at your Build Knowledge notes in your reader's notebook.

2. Make a list of things that inspire people to help in their communities. Include ideas and examples from the texts you read.

3. Use your list to write a song meant to inspire people to help in their communities. Try to include ways that people of different ages can help. Include new vocabulary words in your song.

Think about what you learned in this text set. Fill in the bars on page 11.

# Build Knowledge

# Build Vocabulary

 Write new words you learned about how one person can make a difference. Draw lines and circles for the words you write.

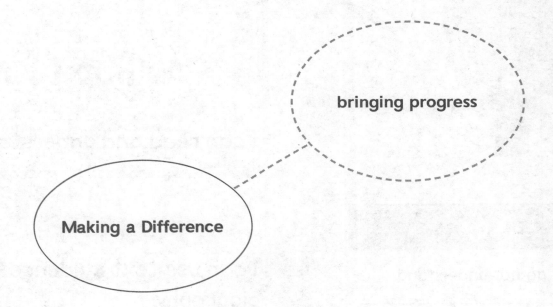

bringing progress

Making a Difference

 Go online to **my.mheducation.com** and read the "The Power Is Yours" Blast. Think about how an individual can make the world a better place. Then blast back your response.

Think about what you already know. Fill in the bars. It's okay if you want more practice.

# What I Know Now

I can read and understand a biography.

1 > 2 > 3 > 4

I can use text evidence to respond to a biography.

1 > 2 > 3 > 4

I know how one person can make a difference.

1 > 2 > 3 > 4

| Key |
| --- |
| **1** = I do not understand. |
| **2** = I understand but need more practice. |
| **3** = I understand. |
| **4** = I understand and can teach someone. |

STOP You will come back to the next page later.

Think about what you learned. Fill in the bars. What progress did you make?

# What I Learned

I can read and understand a biography.

1 > 2 > 3 > 4

I can use text evidence to respond to a biography.

1 > 2 > 3 > 4

I know how one person can make a difference.

1 > 2 > 3 > 4

**My Goal** I can read and understand a biography.

## TAKE NOTES

As you read, make note of interesting words and important information.

# Judy's APPALACHIA

Coal River Folklife Project collection (AFC 1999/008) American Folklife Center, Library of Congress

### Essential Question

How can one person make a difference?

Read about how one person decided to take a stand.

Judy Bonds's six-year-old grandson stood in a creek in West Virginia. He held up a handful of dead fish and asked, "What's wrong with these fish?" All around him dead fish floated belly up in the water. That day became a turning point for Judy Bonds. She decided to fight back against the coal-mining companies that were poisoning her home.

## Marfork, West Virginia

The daughter of a coal miner, Julia "Judy" Bonds was born in Marfork, West Virginia, in 1952. The people of Marfork had been coal miners for generations because coal mining provided people with jobs. Coal gave people the energy they needed to light and warm their homes.

But Marfork wasn't just a place where coal miners lived. Marfork was home to a leafy green valley, or holler, surrounded by the Appalachian Mountains on every side. Judy's family had lived in Marfork for generations. Judy grew up there swimming and fishing in the river. She raised a daughter there.

## Mountaintop Removal Mining

An energy company came to Marfork in the 1990s. It began a process called mountaintop removal mining. Using dynamite, the company blew off the tops of mountains to get at the large amounts of coal underneath. The process was quicker than the old method of digging for coal underground, but it caused many problems. Whole forests were destroyed.

**Judy Bonds spoke out against mountaintop removal mining.**

(b) Bob Bird/AP Images

# BIOGRAPHY

## FIND TEXT EVIDENCE 🔍

**Read**

Paragraph 1

### Author's Perspective

**Underline** the detail that tells what Judy's grandson found in a creek. How does the author describe that day as a turning point for Judy Bonds? Write your answer here.

_____

_____

_____

Paragraphs 2-3

### Reread

**Circle** the details in paragraph 2 that tell why coal mining is important to the people of Marfork.

**Draw a box** around why Marfork is important to Judy.

**Reread**

### Author's Craft

How does the author use a cause-and-effect text structure to organize the information?

**FIND TEXT EVIDENCE**

`Read`

**Paragraphs 1–3**

**Author's Perspective**

**Underline** the effects that mountaintop removal mining had on the people and the land in paragraph 2. How does the author describe Judy's reaction to the pollution? Write your answer here.

_____

_____

**Synonyms and Antonyms**

**Circle** the seventh sentence in paragraph 2. Which two words in the sentence are antonyms? Write the two antonyms below. Then write a synonym for each word.

_____

_____

`Reread`

**Author's Craft**

What inferences can you make about Judy? Use text evidence.

Dust from the explosions filled the air and settled over the towns. Coal sludge, a mixture of mud, chemicals, and coal dust, got into the creeks and rivers.

Pollution from the mountaintop removal mining began making people living in the towns below the mountains sick. In the area where Judy lived, coal sludge flowed into the rivers and streams. People packed up and left. Judy was heartbroken. The land she loved was being **mistreated**. She realized that the valley that had always been her home had been poisoned. No longer a safe place to live, it had become dangerous. Judy, her daughter, and her grandson had to leave.

## Working for Change

Something had to be done about the pollution. Judy decided it was important to **protest** against strip mining and demand that it be stopped. She felt that she must try to keep the area safe for people. She felt **qualified** to talk to groups about the **injustice** of whole towns being forced to move and mountains and forests being destroyed, all because of strip mining. After all, she had grown up in a mining family.

| O **1952** | O **2001** | O **2003** | O **2011** |
|---|---|---|---|
| Judy is born in West Virginia. | Judy's family is forced to leave Marfork Hollow. | Judy is awarded the $150,000 Goldman Environmental Prize. | Judy dies at age 59. |

Judy worked as a volunteer for the Coal River Mountain Watch, a group that fought against mountaintop removal mining. Eventually, she became its executive director. She **registered** to take part in protests against mining companies. At the protests, Judy faced a lot of anger and insults. Many coal miners were not opposed to mountaintop removal mining. They supported it because they needed the jobs to provide for their families. Judy knew it would be impossible to **boycott** the mining companies. The coal miners could not afford to leave their jobs. Instead, she pushed for changes to be made to the mining process. Slowly, small changes were made to protect communities in mining areas. In 2003, Judy was awarded the Goldman Environmental Prize for her efforts as an activist.

## Remembering Judy

Sadly, Judy could not **fulfill** all of her goals. She was diagnosed with cancer and died in January 2011. But her success has provided **encouragement** to other activists. Judy may not have been able to stay in her home, but her work will help preserve and protect the Appalachian Mountains and help others remain in their homes.

**FIND TEXT EVIDENCE** 🔍

Paragraph 1
**Reread**

**Draw a box** around the reason why many people supported mountaintop removal mining. What kind of change did Judy push for? Write your answer here.

_____

_____

_____

Paragraph 2
**Timeline**

What information in paragraph 2 is also listed on the timeline?

_____

_____

Reread
**Author's Craft**

What are some of the words and phrases that the author uses to tell about the work Judy did? What is the author's opinion, or attitude, toward Judy's work?

**Summarize**

Use the central idea and relevant details, as well as your notes, to summarize "Judy's Appalachia."

# Vocabulary

**Use the example sentences to talk with a partner about each word. Then answer the questions.**

### boycott

Joni bought apples instead of grapes after she joined the grape **boycott**.

What would you choose to boycott?

_____

_____

### encouragement

The **encouragement** we needed to win the game came from our fans.

What kind of encouragement do you give others?

_____

_____

### fulfill

Jules got to **fulfill** his dream of performing in the school talent show.

What dream would you like to fulfill one day?

_____

_____

### injustice

The children felt that it was an **injustice** that they were not allowed on the roller coaster because they were too short.

How are *injustice* and *justice* related?

_____

_____

### mistreated

Tomas felt that the dog's first owner had hurt and **mistreated** her.

What is an antonym for *mistreated*?

_____

_____

**Build Your Word List** Reread the third paragraph on page 39. Circle the word *leafy*. Look up the word in a thesaurus. In your reader's notebook, write down words with similar meanings. Then, write a sentence using one of your synonyms.

**protest**

The children decided to **protest** the cutting down of trees in the forest.

What is a synonym for *protest*?

_____

_____

**qualified**

Doctor Smith and the nurse are **qualified** to tell what treatment the boy needs.

What would you need to do to be qualified for a spelling bee?

_____

_____

**registered**

The woman gave her address so that she could be **registered** to vote.

Why is it important to be registered to vote?

_____

_____

# Synonyms and Antonyms

Authors may use synonyms and antonyms to help you figure out an unfamiliar word. Synonyms are words with similar meanings. Antonyms have opposite meanings.

## FIND TEXT EVIDENCE

*In the text below, the word* supported *helps me understand the word* opposed. *I know that* supported *means "was in favor of." This will help me figure out what* opposed *means.*

Many coal miners were not opposed to mountaintop removal mining. They supported it because they needed the jobs to provide for their families.

**Your Turn** With a partner, list synonyms and antonyms for these words from the text:

**leafy,** page 39 _____

_____

**preserve,** page 41 _____

CHECK IN  1  2  3  4

Aimin Tang/R+/Getty Images

# Reread

When you read an informational text, you may come across information and facts that are new to you. As you read "Judy's Appalachia," reread sections of text to make sure you understand and remember the information.

 **FIND TEXT EVIDENCE**

You may not be sure what mountaintop removal mining is. Reread the fourth paragraph of "Judy's Appalachia" on page 39.

> **Quick Tip**
>
> When you reread an informational text, remember to slow down. Read each sentence carefully and make sure you understand the sentence before you read the next one.

Page 39

> An energy company came to Marfork in the 1990s. It began a process called mountaintop removal mining. Using dynamite, the company blew off the tops of mountains to get at the large amounts of coal underneath. The process was quicker than the old method of digging for coal underground, but it caused many problems. Whole forests were destroyed.

*I read that an energy company started a different process of getting coal. The company blows off the top of a mountain to get to the coal underneath.*

 **Your Turn** Why did Judy Bonds leave Marfork? Read page 40 of "Judy's Appalachia" to answer the question. As you read, remember to use the strategy Reread.

_____

_____

CHECK IN 1 2 3 4

# Timeline

The selection "Judy's Appalachia" is a biography.

A biography

- is the story of a real person's life written by another person
- usually presents events in chronological order
- may include text features such as timelines and photographs

### Readers to Writers

Timelines help readers see the chronological order, or time order, of important events in a person's life. When would you use a timeline in your writing?

## 🔍 FIND TEXT EVIDENCE

*You can tell "Judy's Appalachia" is a biography because the text describes a real person. The events in Judy's life are presented in chronological order. The story includes text features.*

Page 40

Dust from the explosions filled the air and settled over the towns. Coal sludge, a mixture of mud, chemicals, and coal dust, got into the creeks and rivers.

Pollution from the mountaintop removal mining began making people living in the towns below the mountains sick. In the area where Judy lived, coal sludge flowed into the rivers and streams. People packed up and left. Judy was heartbroken. The land she loved was being **mistreated**. She realized that the valley that had always been her home had been poisoned. No longer a safe place to live, it had become dangerous. Judy, her daughter, and her grandson had to leave.

### Working for Change

Something had to be done about the pollution. Judy decided it was important to **protest** against strip mining and demand that it be stopped. She felt that she must try to keep the area safe for people. She felt **qualified** to talk to groups about the **injustice** of whole towns being forced to move and mountains and forests being destroyed, all because of strip mining. After all, she had grown up in a mining family.

| 1952 | 2001 | 2003 | 2011 |
|------|------|------|------|
| Judy is born in West Virginia. | Judy's family is forced to leave Marfork Hollow. | Judy is awarded the $150,000 Goldman Environmental Prize. | Judy dies at age 59. |

## Timeline

A timeline is a kind of diagram that shows events in the order in which they took place.

👥 **COLLABORATE** **Your Turn** Review and discuss the events on the timeline. Why did the author include the timeline? How is the information helpful?

_____

_____

_____

_____

CHECK IN  1  2  3  4

# Author's Perspective

An author's perspective is the attitude an author has toward something or someone. Look for details in the text, such as the reasons and evidence the author chooses to present. This will help you to figure out the author's perspective.

 **FIND TEXT EVIDENCE**

*When I reread the first paragraph on page 39, I can look for details that reveal the author's perspective on Judy Bonds.*

| Details |
|---|
| Judy sees her grandson in a creek surrounded by dead fish. |
| Judy decides to fight the mining companies. They are poisoning her home. |

| Author's Perspective |
|---|
| The author admires Judy Bonds for taking a stand against the coal-mining companies. |

**COLLABORATE**

**Your Turn** Reread "Judy's Appalachia." Look for two more details that help support the author's perspective, and list them in your graphic organizer on page 47.

CHECK IN ▶ 1 ▷ 2 ▷ 3 ▷ 4 ▷

| Details |
| --- |
|  |
|  |
|  |

↓

| Author's Perspective |
| --- |
|  |

# Respond to Reading

COLLABORATE

Discuss the prompt below. Use your notes and text evidence to support your ideas.

How do Judy's actions help readers understand why it is important to stand up for what is right? _____

_____

_____

_____

_____

_____

_____

_____

_____

_____

_____

_____

## Quick Tip

Use these sentence starters to discuss the prompt.

- *Judy Bonds realized she needed to protest against mountaintop removal mining when . . .*

- *Some effects of mountaintop removal mining were . . .*

- *Judy Bonds felt qualified to talk about coal mining because . . .*

## Grammar Connections

As you write your response, put quotation marks around words and phrases that come from the text. Remember that punctuation at the end of the quote goes inside the quotation marks.

**CHECK IN** 〉 1 〉 2 〉 3 〉 4 〉

# People Who Made a Difference

COLLABORATE

As you have learned, one person can make a difference. Follow the research process to make a book cover for a biography of a significant person who made a difference in US history. Include information about how the person made a difference. Work with a partner.

**Step 1** **Set a Goal** Scan books or websites to find people who have made a difference. Choose a person who really interests you. Then create a list of questions you want your research to answer. For example, when did this person live? What were his or her major achievements? How did this person make a difference?

**Step 2** **Identify Sources** Find books, magazines, and websites that have information about your chosen person.

**Step 3** **Find and Record Information** When taking notes, it is important to paraphrase, or restate, the information you find in your own words. That way you can avoid plagiarism. Record all the sources that you used.

**Step 4** **Organize and Synthesize Information** Organize your information. Write about the person's achievements for the inside flap of the book cover. On the back cover, write a summary telling why this person made a difference.

**Step 5** **Create and Present** Create your final book cover. Include a title. Think about ways to share your book cover with the class.

Paraphrase this description of educator Mary McLeod Bethune.
*Bethune was an influential educator and social activist who championed black education, civil rights, and women's rights.*

_____

_____

_____

_____

_____

Library of Congress Prints & Photographs Division [LC-DIG-fsa-8d125101]

**CHECK IN** ❯ 1 ❯ 2 ❯ 3 ❯ 4 ❯

# Delivering Justice

*Literature Anthology: pages 196–213*

 **How does the author help you visualize how Westley and Grandma were treated at Levy's?**

 **Talk About It** Reread page 199 of the **Literature Anthology**. Talk to your partner about what happened to Westley and Grandma at Levy's.

**Cite Text Evidence** What words does the author use to help you picture what happened? Write text evidence here.

 **Make Inferences**

Think about how the saleswoman treats Westley's grandma on page 199. Then think about Grandma's words and actions. What inferences can you make about Grandma?

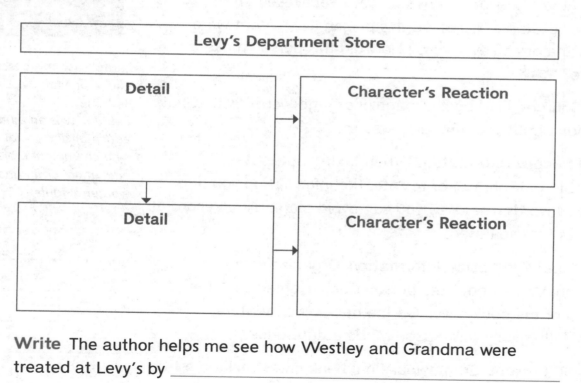

| Levy's Department Store |
|---|

| Detail | Character's Reaction |
|---|---|
| | |

| Detail | Character's Reaction |
|---|---|
| | |

**Write** The author helps me see how Westley and Grandma were treated at Levy's by _____

_____

_____

CHECK IN 1 2 3 4

**How do you know what kind of person Westley is?**

**Talk About It** Reread page 203 of the **Literature Anthology**. Turn to your partner and talk about Westley's role in voter registration.

**Cite Text Evidence** What do Westley's actions show about his character? What inferences can you make about Westley? Cite text evidence in the chart.

| How Westley Helps | What This Shows |
|---|---|
| | |

**Write** The author helps me understand what kind of person Westley is by

_____

_____

_____

### Quick Tip

Use these sentence starters when you talk about Westley.

- *The author tells how Westley . . .*
- *Westley went with people to . . .*
- *This detail helps me see that . . .*

### Readers to Writers

The author does not tell the reader that Westley is a caring person. Instead, he describes Westley's actions to help people register to vote.

In your writing, use the words and actions of your characters to show what they are like. For example, *Tanya was happy about going to Peru.* To show more about the character, you could write: *Tanya hugged her mother and danced around the kitchen.* The reader can infer that Tanya is happy.

**CHECK IN** 1 2 3 4

**?** How does the illustration help you understand what a boycott is?

**Talk About It** Look at the illustration on **Literature Anthology** page 208. Reread page 209. Discuss what the people are doing.

**Cite Text Evidence** What clues in the illustration and the text help you understand what a boycott is? Write evidence in the chart.

| Illustration Clues | Text Clues | How They Help |
|---|---|---|
|  |  |  |

**Write** The author uses the illustration to help me understand that a boycott is _____

_____

_____

**Quick Tip**

Use these sentence starters to help you talk about the illustration on page 208.

- *The people in the picture are . . .*
- *The people are carrying . . .*
- *There is a pile of . . .*

 **Synthesize Information**

Combine the information from the text you have read so far and the illustration to develop your understanding. Why are people boycotting the shops on Broughton Street? Look at all the charge cards in the illustration. Why might this boycott be an effective way to create change?

CHECK IN ⟩ 1 ⟩ 2 ⟩ 3 ⟩ 4 ⟩

# Respond to Reading

COLLABORATE

Discuss the prompt below. Use your notes and text evidence to support your response.

What can readers learn from Westley Law and his actions?

_____

_____

_____

_____

_____

_____

_____

_____

_____

_____

_____

_____

_____

_____

## Quick Tip

Use these sentence starters to talk about and cite text evidence.

- *Westley Law needed to help people register to vote because . . .*

- *People boycotted shops on Broughton Street because . . .*

- *Westley Law worked with other members of the NAACP to . . .*

CHECK IN  1  2  3  4

# Keeping Freedom in the Family

Literature Anthology:
pages 216–219

1   As I held on to my father's hand, we joined the line of people chanting and walking back and forth in a picket line in front of Lawrence Hospital. The year was 1965, and the hospital workers needed more money and better working conditions. So there we were on a cold Saturday afternoon to protest. When I looked up, I saw soldiers on the roof of the hospital. I squeezed Daddy's hand a little tighter. The soldiers were there to protect us, he said. We were American citizens, and we had the right to gather and to protest. I raised my picket sign as high as I could. I wasn't afraid. I had Daddy and the American Constitution to protect me.

**Circle** words that describe the picket line.

**Underline** why Nora and her family are participating in the protest. Write the reason here.

_____

_____

_____

_____

**COLLABORATE**

Talk with a partner about how Nora feels. **Draw a box** around text evidence that supports your ideas.

1     When four black girls were killed in a church bombing in Alabama, we realized that the fight for change would be hard, long, and dangerous. Mom and Dad encouraged us to think about how we could protest the bombing. Some people said we should boycott Christmas. This was our first Christmas in the new house, and the spirit of giving was important to us.

2     So, instead of boycotting Christmas, our family decided to boycott Christmas shopping. Instead of buying gifts, our family gave the money to civil rights groups. Guy, La Verne, and I gave each other gifts we had made with our own hands. And when the time came to hang the home-made paper holiday chain, I wrote the names of the girls in the last four loops. In our own small way, we learned the true meaning of giving.

3     When we gathered for dinner that night, we said a special prayer for the girls and for our country—and I knew that Christmas at the Davis house would never be the same.

Reread paragraph 1. **Underline** how the author helps you understand that protesting the bombing was important to her family. Then reread paragraph 2. **Circle** how Nora and her family chose to protest.

COLLABORATE

Reread paragraph 3. Talk with a partner about why "Christmas at the Davis house would never be the same." **Put checkmarks** in the margin beside the text evidence that supports this.

**How does the author help you visualize what it was like to walk in a picket line?**

**Quick Tip**

Look for details in the text that describe sounds, sights, and actions. Use these sensory details to help you visualize the event from the text.

COLLABORATE

**Talk About It** Reread the excerpt on page 54. Talk with a partner about what happened at the protest.

**Cite Text Evidence** What words help you picture how walking in the picket line felt to Nora? Write text evidence in the web.

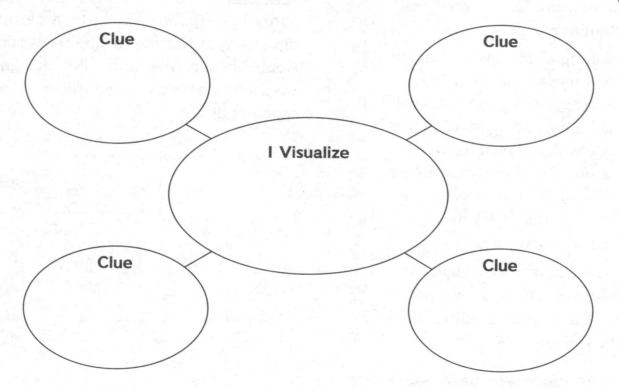

Clue

Clue

I Visualize

Clue

Clue

**Write** I can visualize what the picket line was like because the author

_____

_____

_____

CHECK IN  1  2  3  4

# Author's Purpose

An author's purpose is the main reason he or she writes something. Authors write to persuade, inform, or entertain. When you read a text, think about what the author wants the readers to know and why.

## FIND TEXT EVIDENCE

In paragraph 1 on page 54 of "Keeping Freedom in the Family," the author gives information about her and her father joining a protest to support hospital workers. This helps readers understand right away that the author comes from a family that cares about justice.

> As I held on to my father's hand, we joined the line of people chanting and walking back and forth in a picket line in front of Lawrence Hospital. The year was 1965, and the hospital workers needed more money and better working conditions.

**Your Turn** Reread the first paragraph on page 218 in the **Literature Anthology**. What is the author's purpose for including this paragraph? Be specific. What does the author want readers to know?

_____

_____

_____

**Quick Tip**

While autobiographies might be written in entertaining ways, usually the authors' main purpose is to give information about their experiences, ideas, and the time period they are writing about.

Wuttichok Panichiwarapun/Shutterstock.com

CHECK IN ▷ 1 ⟩ 2 ⟩ 3 ⟩ 4

COLLABORATE

**?** How is the information in *Delivering Justice,* "Keeping Freedom in the Family," and "Paul Revere's Ride" similar? What does this information help you understand about how one person can make a difference?

**Talk About It** With a partner, read the poem. Talk about what Paul Revere plans to do if the British invade.

**Cite Text Evidence** **Circle** words and phrases that describe the actions of Paul Revere's plan. **Underline** the words that show what the people will do if Paul Revere spreads the alarm.

**Write** The selections that I read and the poem help me understand that one person can make a difference by _____

_____

_____

_____

_____

_____

_____

_____

_____

_____

_____

_____

Quick Tip

Use these sentence starters to talk about the selections you have read.

• *Westley Law made a difference by . . .*

• *Nora Davis Day learned . . .*

• *Paul Revere made a difference by . . .*

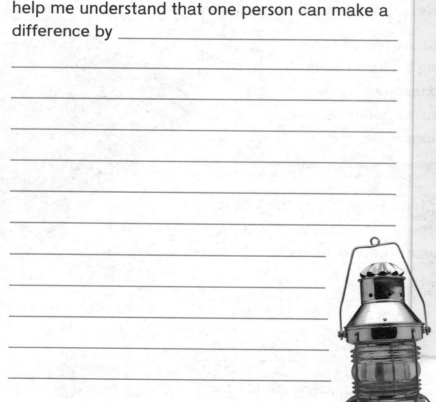

from **Paul Revere's Ride**

He said to his friend, "If the British march
By land or sea from the town to-night,
Hang a lantern aloft in the belfry-arch
Of the North-Church-tower, as a signal-light,—
One if by land, and two if by sea;
And I on the opposite shore will be,
Ready to ride and spread the alarm
Through every Middlesex village and farm,
For the country-folk to be up and to arm."

— Henry Wadsworth Longfellow

**CHECK IN** 1 2 3 4

George Doyle/SuperStock

My Goal: **I know how one person can make a difference.**

## Write an Essay

Think about what you learned about how one person can make a difference. Why is it important for people to believe they can make a difference?

1. Look at your Build Knowledge notes in your reader's notebook.

2. Write down your ideas about what can happen when people believe they can make a difference. Use examples from the texts to support your ideas.

3. Use your ideas to write an essay explaining why it is important to know that one person can make a difference. Use new vocabulary words in your essay.

Think about what you learned in this text set. Fill in the bars on page 37.

# Build Knowledge

**Essential Question**

In what ways can advances in science be helpful or harmful?

# Build Vocabulary

Write new words you learned about advances in science and growing food. Draw lines and circles for the words you write.

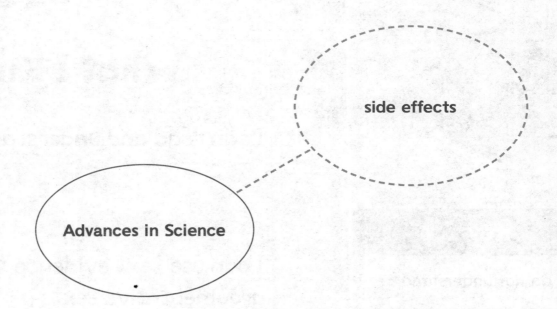

side effects

Advances in Science

Go online to **my.mheducation.com** and read the "Fertilizers: The Good and the Bad" Blast. What is your opinion about using fertilizers? Blast back your response.

Think about what you already know. Fill in the bars. Let's keep learning!

| Key |
|-----|
| **1** = I do not understand. |
| **2** = I understand but need more practice. |
| **3** = I understand. |
| **4** = I understand and can teach someone. |

# What I Know Now

I can read and understand argumentative text.

1 > 2 > 3 > 4 >

I can use text evidence to respond to argumentative text.

1 > 2 > 3 > 4 >

I know in what ways science can be helpful or harmful.

1 > 2 > 3 > 4 >

**STOP** You will come back to the next page later.

Think about what you learned. Fill in the bars. Keep working hard!

# What I Learned

I can read and understand argumentative text.

| 1 | 2 | 3 | 4 |

I can use text evidence to respond to argumentative text.

| 1 | 2 | 3 | 4 |

I know in what ways science can be helpful or harmful.

| 1 | 2 | 3 | 4 |

**My Goal** I can read and understand argumentative text.

## TAKE NOTES

As you read, make note of interesting words and important information.

_____

_____

_____

_____

_____

_____

_____

_____

_____

_____

_____

_____

TIME for **KiDS**

### Essential Question

**?**

**In what ways can advances in science be helpful or harmful?**

Read about how science has helped to change food crops.

John Lamb/The Image Bank/Getty Images

# Food Fight

## Is It Safe to Interfere with Mother Nature?

Some scientists use a technique called genetic modification to make "superior" food crops. It involves altering a seed's genes. Genes are the "instruction codes" that all living things have inside their cells. A seed's genetic code sets what **characteristics** it will **inherit** when it grows into a plant, such as how big it will grow and the nutrients it will contain.

For thousands of years, farmers made crops better by crossbreeding plants. They would add pollen from the sweetest melon plants to the flowers of plants that produced the biggest melons. This process would make new plants with big, sweet melons. But this crossbreeding process does not always work, and its cycle can take years to get good results.

But advances in gene science have created shortcuts. Using new tools, scientists can put a gene from one living thing into another.

That living thing could be a plant, a bacterium, a virus, or even an animal. These foods are called genetically modified foods, or GM foods. The goal of GM foods is to create foods that can survive insects or harsh conditions or can grow faster. But are these **advancements** in **agriculture** good for us?

Annabelle Breakey/Digital Vision/Getty Images

## ARGUMENTATIVE TEXT

### FIND TEXT EVIDENCE

**Read**
Paragraphs 1–2
**Greek Roots**

The Greek root *techn-* means "skill" or "method." **Circle** a word with the Greek root *techn-* in it. What other words do you know that have this Greek root?

___

**Author's Claim**
**Underline** the author's claim about the effect of crossbreeding on plants.

Paragraphs 3–4
**Reread**

**Draw a box** around the text that tells what kinds of living things scientists take genes from.

**Reread**
**Author's Craft**

What is the author's purpose for questioning if the advancements in agriculture will be good for us?

## FIND TEXT EVIDENCE

**Read**

Paragraphs 1–3

### Author's Claim

**Underline** the sentence that tells you what the author thinks about Bt corn.

### Reread

**Draw a box** around text that tells why the author thinks genetically modified rice is a good thing.

### Sidebar
### Headings

Write the headings shown in the sidebar on the lines below. **Circle** how each food was improved.

_____

_____

**Reread**

### Author's Craft

What facts does the author use to support the argument for GM foods?

TIME For KiDS

## Support for Superfoods

**S**cientists believe the new techniques can create crops with a **resistance** to pests and disease. Bt corn is a genetically modified corn.

It has an insect-killing gene that comes from a bacterium. Farmers who grow Bt corn can use fewer chemicals while they grow their crops. That is good for the environment.

**Disease-resistant GM potatoes were introduced in the 1990s.**

Some superfoods are extra nutritious. Golden rice has been genetically modified with three different genes. One gene is a form of bacterium. The other two are from daffodils. The new genes help the rice to make a nutrient that prevents some forms of blindness.

## Superfoods

**These foods may seem common. But did you know that the genetically modified versions have special powers?**

### Rice

Rice contains phytic acid. Too much of this acid can be bad for people. A new type of rice has been bred with a low level of phytic acid.

### Salmon

To create supersized salmon, scientists changed the gene that controls growth. The genetically altered salmon grow twice as fast as their wild cousins.

### Tomatoes

Genetically engineered tomatoes can be picked when they are ripe and still not bruise when shipped. One food company tried to use an Arctic flounder fish gene to create a tomato that could survive frost. The fish-tomato did not succeed.

## Map

**MAP KEY**
Percentage of people that are not getting enough food

- ☐ Over 35%
- ☐ 20-34%
- ☐ 10-19%
- ☐ 5-9%
- ☐ Less than 5%
- ☐ Not enough data

*(Map of Africa with countries labeled: Western Sahara, Morocco, Tunisia, Algeria, Libya, Egypt, Cape Verde, Mauritania, Mali, Niger, Chad, Sudan, Eritrea, Gambia, Guinea-Bissau, Senegal, Burkina Faso, Guinea, Benin, Nigeria, Djibouti, Sierra Leone, Côte D'ivoire, Ghana, Togo, Cameroon, Central African Republic, South Sudan, Ethiopia, Somalia, Liberia, Equatorial Guinea, São Tomé & Principe, Gabon, Congo, Democratic Republic Of The Congo, Uganda, Kenya, Rwanda, Burundi, Cabinda (Angola), Tanzania, Seychelles, Angola, Malawi, Comoros, Zambia, Zimbabwe, Mozambique, Madagascar, Mauritius, Namibia, Botswana, Swaziland, South Africa, Lesotho)*

## Safety Issues

**M**any people have **disagreed** that GM foods are a good idea. They worry that GM foods will hurt the environment and humans. One concern is that plants with new genes will crossbreed with weeds to make pesticide-resistant weeds. Another concern is that GM foods may trigger allergies.

Genetically modified crops are **prevalent** in the United States. But some people will not buy them because of health **concerns**. GM foods can leave foreign material inside us, causing lifelong problems.

As a result, many companies avoid GM foods.

## The Long Term

**G**enetically modified foods pollute the environment forever because it is impossible to fully clean up a contaminated gene pool. It is important to keep researching GM foods because these types of foods can create dangerous side effects.

**Summarize**

Use your notes and the map to help you summarize "Food Fight."

# Vocabulary

**Use the example sentences to talk with a partner about each word. Then answer the questions.**

### advancements
The latest **advancements** in technology have improved cell phones.

What advancements in technology have you heard about recently?

_____

_____

### agriculture
Jaime studied **agriculture** to learn how to grow more crops on his farm.

Why is agriculture important?

_____

_____

### characteristics
Feathers and wings are two **characteristics** of a bird.

What characteristics does a cat have?

_____

_____

### concerns
I had **concerns** about my dog's health.

What have you had concerns about?

_____

_____

### disagreed
The brothers **disagreed** about whose turn it was to wash the dishes.

What have you disagreed with someone about?

_____

_____

**Build Your Word List** Pick one of the interesting words you noted on page 64 and look up its meaning in a print or digital dictionary. Then in your reader's notebook make a word web with synonyms, antonyms, and related words.

**inherit**

Mom hopes the baby will **inherit** her red hair.

What other characteristics can we inherit from our parents?

_____

_____

**prevalent**

Snowstorms are **prevalent** in the Northeast in the winter.

What kind of weather is prevalent where you live in springtime?

_____

_____

_____

**resistance**

Brushing and flossing your teeth can build up a **resistance** to tooth decay.

How can you build up a resistance to an illness?

_____

_____

## Greek Roots

Knowing Greek roots can help you figure out the meanings of unfamiliar words. Here are some common Greek roots that may help you as you read "Food Fight."

*gen* = race, kind     *techn* = art, skill, method
*agr* = field        *chron* = time

### 🔍 FIND TEXT EVIDENCE

*When I read the word* cycle *on page 65, I know the Greek root* cycl *means "circle." Cycle* must mean "a series of events that repeat regularly."

**But this crossbreeding process does not always work, and its cycle can take years to get good results.**

**Your Turn** Use Greek roots and context clues to find the meanings of the following words from "Food Fight."

**gene,** page 65 _____

_____

**agriculture,** page 65 _____

_____

CHECK IN ▶ 1 ⟩ 2 ⟩ 3 ⟩ 4 ⟩

# Reread

In an argumentative text, an author makes a claim about a topic and provides facts to support the claim. The author wants to convince readers to agree with his or her claim. Reread the text to make sure you understand the claim and supporting facts. This will help you form an opinion about the claim.

 **FIND TEXT EVIDENCE**

You may not be sure about identifying a claim and a supporting fact. Reread the last paragraph on page 66 of "Food Fight," which makes a claim and gives a supporting fact.

Page 66

    Some superfoods are extra nutritious. Golden rice has been genetically modified with three different genes. One gene is a form of bacterium. The other two are from daffodils. The new genes help the rice to make a nutrient that prevents some forms of blindness.

*I read the claim that golden rice is extra nutritious. The fact that supports the claim is that golden rice has been genetically modified with three different genes. The new genes help the rice make a nutrient that prevents some forms of blindness.*

**Your Turn** Explain how the author supports the claim that GM foods are not a good idea. Reread "Safety Issues" on page 67 to answer the question. As you read, remember to use the strategy Reread.

_____

_____

CHECK IN 1 2 3 4

# Maps and Headings

"Food Fight" is an argumentative text that presents opposing claims, or arguments, about a topic. The claims are supported by reasons and evidence. Argumentative texts may include text features such as maps and headings to clarify or further support claims.

 **FIND TEXT EVIDENCE**

*"Food Fight" is an argumentative text that gives reasons for and against GM foods. It includes text features, such as headings and maps, to help support the author's claims.*

**Readers to Writers**

Writers use maps to give readers additional facts about the topic. They use headings to help organize the text. All the details under a heading are related. How can you use these text features in your writing?

Page 67

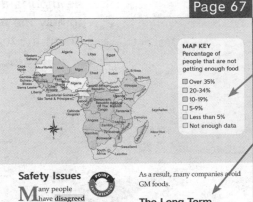

**MAP KEY**
Percentage of people that are not getting enough food

☐ Over 35%
☐ 20-34%
☐ 10-19%
☐ 5-9%
☐ Less than 5%
☐ Not enough data

**Safety Issues**

 Many people have **disagreed** that GM foods are a good idea. They worry that GM foods will hurt the environment and humans. One concern is that plants with new genes will crossbreed with weeds to make pesticide-resistant weeds. Another concern is that GM foods may trigger allergies.

Genetically modified crops are **prevalent** in the United States. But some people will not buy them because of health **concerns**. GM foods can leave foreign material inside us, causing lifelong problems.

As a result, many companies avoid GM foods.

**The Long Term**

Genetically modified foods pollute the environment forever because it is impossible to fully clean up a contaminated gene pool. It is important to keep researching GM foods because these types of foods can create dangerous side effects.

**Summarize**

**?** Use your notes and the map to help you summarize "Food Fight."

**Maps**
Maps show geographic locations of specific areas of the world. They usually include a map key and a compass rose.

**Headings**
Headings tell you what the section is mostly about.

**COLLABORATE** **Your Turn** Find two other text features in "Food Fight." Tell what information you learned from each feature.

_____

_____

_____

CHECK IN ▷ 1 ▷ 2 ▷ 3 ▷ 4

# Author's Claim

Authors use reasons and evidence to support their claims, or arguments. To identify or better understand an author's claim, look for relevant details, including what the author thinks and feels. Then look for what the details have in common. What do the details help you understand about the claim?

 **FIND TEXT EVIDENCE**

*When I reread page 66 of "Food Fight," I can identify relevant details about the topic of GM foods to help me understand the author's claim.*

| Details |
| --- |
| Farmers who grow Bt corn use fewer chemicals. |
| Using fewer chemicals is good for the environment. |
| Some GM foods have been created to be extra nutritious. |

| Author's Claim |
| --- |
|  |

 **Your Turn** Reread page 67. Find relevant details in the section and list them in your graphic organizer on page 73. What is the author's claim?

**Quick Tip**

The details an author includes in a text should support the author's claim. As you look for details, ask yourself what idea the details support.

Details include the use of positive or negative words. Identify words and phrases that show the author's strong feelings for or against an idea. Positive and negative words, such as *good, harmful,* or *important,* are clues to how the author feels about the topic.

CHECK IN 1 2 3 4

| Details |
| --- |
| |
| |
| |

↓

| Author's Claim |
| --- |
| |

# Respond to Reading

Discuss the prompt below. Use your notes and text evidence to support your ideas.

What does reading opposing claims, or arguments, about genetically modified food help you understand?

_____

_____

_____

_____

_____

_____

_____

_____

_____

_____

_____

_____

_____

_____

## Quick Tip

Use these sentence starters to discuss the text and organize your ideas.

- *One reason why some people are opposed to genetically modified food is . . .*

- *Benefits of genetically modifying food include . . .*

- *Reading both sides of the argument helped me to . . .*

## Grammar Connections

As you write your response, make sure that the subjects of your sentences agree with your verbs.

**Singular** The farmer is growing corn.

**Plural** The farmers are growing corn.

**CHECK IN** ⟩ 1 ⟩ 2 ⟩ 3 ⟩ 4 ⟩

## Advances in Farming Technology

Create a multimedia slideshow that tells about a technological advance in farming, including its effect on the environment. Work with a group and follow the research process to create your slideshow.

**Step 1** **Set a Goal** As part of your research, you'll find and choose a technological advance in farming to write about. List questions you want your research to answer.

**Step 2** **Identify Sources** Scan, or quickly look at, books or websites to find examples of technological advances in farming. Choose one. Write it here. _____

_____

**Step 3** **Find and Record Information** Take notes in your own words. Look for images and audio you might want to use. Cite where your information came from and create a list of sources.

**Step 4** **Organize and Synthesize Information** Analyze your information, including audio and visuals. Decide what you will include in your slideshow and how you want to organize it.

**Step 5** **Create and Present** Create your slideshow and decide how to present it to the class.

### Quick Tip

Technological advances in farming can include both recent and older technological advances. Remember to look for the effect the technological advances have had on the environment.

Here are some categories of technological advances in farming:

- Farm Equipment
- Treatment and Care of Animals
- Pesticides
- Treating Soil to Grow Things in
- Types of Crops

CHECK IN  1  2  3  4

# A New Kind of Corn

 **What is the author's purpose for including a pie chart to show how corn is used?**

*Literature Anthology: pages 220–223*

**Talk About It** Reread the sidebar on page 221 of the **Literature Anthology**. With a partner, analyze the pie chart. Talk about how the information in the chart is related to all of the text on the page.

**Cite Text Evidence** In what ways does the information in the text and the pie chart help you understand more about Bt corn? Find evidence and write it in the chart.

 **Evaluating Information**

In an argumentative text, the author must provide evidence to support his or her claim. How would you check the information in the pie chart to see if it is reliable?

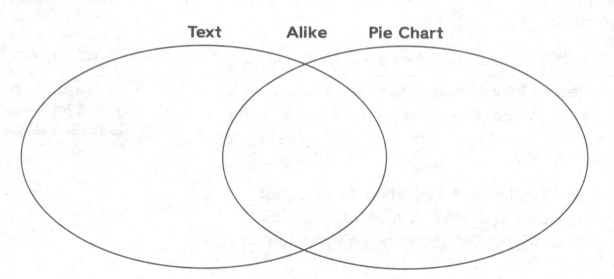

Text        Alike        Pie Chart

**Write** The author uses the sidebar with the pie chart to _____

_____

_____

CHECK IN ▷ 1 ▷ 2 ▷ 3 ▷ 4 ▷

**?** How do the authors of both argumentative text articles help you understand what they think?

**Talk About It** Reread the two articles on pages 222 and 223 of the **Literature Anthology**. Turn to a partner and talk about the different perspectives and claims presented in the articles.

**Cite Text Evidence** What relevant details help you understand the central, or main, claim of the farmer and the consumer? Write text evidence in the chart.

> **Quick Tip**
>
> You can use these sentence starters when you talk about the two different perspectives.
>
> - *The farmer explains that planting Bt corn has . . .*
> - *The consumer explains that Bt corn . . .*

| Bt Corn Is Better | Bt Corn Could Be Bad |
|---|---|
|  |  |
|  |  |
|  |  |
| Author's Claim | Author's Claim |

**Write** The intended audience for the argumentative articles is_____

_____

# Respond to Reading

Discuss the prompt below. Use your notes and text evidence to support your ideas.

What is your opinion about Bt corn? Why do you feel that way?

_____

_____

_____

_____

_____

_____

_____

_____

_____

_____

_____

_____

_____

### Quick Tip

Use these sentence starters to discuss the text and to organize ideas.

- *Some farmers plant Bt corn because . . .*
- *Some people are worried about . . .*
- *I think . . . because . . .*

CHECK IN 〉 1 〉 2 〉 3 〉 4 〉

# The Pick of the Patch

*Literature Anthology:*
*pages 224–225*

1.     This world record-breaking pumpkin tipped the scales at more than 1,810 pounds. What is the secret to growing a giant gourd? According to record-breaker Chris Stevens, "Sunshine, rain, cow manure, fish [fertilizer], and seaweed." Read on for a recipe you can recreate at home.

2.     Growing a giant pumpkin takes knowledge and skill. Follow these six simple steps to grow your own great gourd.

   **1. Study up on seeds.**

   Some popular pumpkin seeds that get big results include Prizewinner Hybrid, Atlantic Giant, Mammoth Gold, and Big Max. Many are sold online for just $1.

   **2. Take your time.**

   Giant pumpkins need time to grow. May is a good month to plant seeds in a pot. Let them make advancements in that safe space before you transplant them outside. Plant them in good quality soil and fertilize them well.

Reread paragraph 1. **Underline** how the author gets you interested in reading more about how to grow a giant pumpkin.

Reread paragraph 2. **Circle** what it takes to grow a giant pumpkin. Write the answers here.

_____

_____

_____

_____

**COLLABORATE**

Talk with a partner about how the author helps you understand how to grow a giant pumpkin. **Draw a box** around how the author helps you understand what each step is going to be about.

**?** How does the way the author organizes the information in this selection help you understand what it takes to grow a great pumpkin?

**Talk About It** Reread the excerpt on page 79. Talk with a partner about what you learned from the author about how to get started growing a big pumpkin.

**Cite Text Evidence** What does the author do that helps you understand how to grow a 1,810-pound pumpkin? Write text evidence in the chart.

Reread the excerpt on page 79.

| What the Author Does | How It Helps |
|---|---|
|  |  |
|  |  |
|  |  |

**Write** The author helps me understand how to grow a great pumpkin by

_____

_____

_____

_____

> ## Quick Tip
>
> These sentence starters will help you discuss the steps to growing a giant pumpkin.
>
> - *In Step 1, we learn about some popular pumpkin seeds, which are . . .*
> - *In Step 2, we learn the best month to plant . . .*

CHECK IN  1  2  3  4

Blend Images/Image Source

# Sequence

Authors often use a sequence text structure to help readers better understand how to do something. A sequence text structure presents information as a series of instructions or steps in a process. Often the steps are numbered or the text has signal words that show the order in which something happens, such as *first, next, then,* and *finally.*

## FIND TEXT EVIDENCE

On page 225 of "The Pick of the Patch" in the **Literature Anthology**, the author gives a brief introduction that explains how many steps it will take to grow a large pumpkin.

> Growing a giant pumpkin takes knowledge and skill. Follow these <u>six simple steps</u> to grow your own great gourd.

**Your Turn** Reread Steps 5 and 6 on page 225 of the **Literature Anthology**.

• How can you give a pumpkin a better chance to grow? Write it here.

_____

_____

• How long should you water and fertilize pumpkins? Write it here.

_____

_____

## Readers to Writers

Texts that use a sequence structure include recipes, instructions for how to play games or build something, and science experiments.

When you use a sequence text structure, choose precise words that clearly explain what to do. Write a list of steps to make it easy for readers to follow. You can begin each step with an imperative (command) verb, such as *take, put, cut,* or *open.* Think of a word that will answer the reader's question: "What do I do next?"

How is the information in the song "Did You Feed My Cow?" similar to the information in "A New Kind of Corn" and "The Pick of the Patch"?

**Talk About It** Read the lyrics of the song. How is the information presented? What can readers learn from the song?

**Cite Text Evidence** **Circle** the lyrics that show what is being asked. Then **underline** the responses to the questions. Think about the kind of details that are in both the questions and the responses.

**Write** The information in the song and selections all tells about _____

_____

_____

_____

_____

_____

## "Did You Feed My Cow?"

(lyrics)

Did you feed my cow?
(Yes, Ma-am)

Could you tell me how?
(Yes, Ma-am)

What did you feed her?
(Corn and hay)

What did you feed her?
(Corn and hay)

Did you milk her good?
(Yes, Ma-am)

Now did you milk her like you should?
(Yes, Ma-am)

How did you milk her?
(Squish, squish, squish)

How did you milk her?
(Squish, squish, squish)

**My Goal** I know ways that advances in science can be helpful or harmful.

# Create a Comic Strip

You read about agriculture advances in science and the effects of those advances. What is your opinion about those advances?

**1** Look at your Build Knowledge notes in your reader's notebook.

**2** Write a pro and con list about agricultural advances. Use text evidence to support your opinions.

**3** Use your list to make a comic strip that shows your opinion about the agricultural advances. Try to use new vocabulary words in your comic strip.

Think about what you learned in this text set. Fill in the bars on page 63.

Think about what you already know. Fill in the bars. It's important to keep learning.

## Key

1 = I do not understand.

2 = I understand but need more practice.

3 = I understand.

4 = I understand and can teach someone.

# What I Know Now

I can write an argumentative essay.

| 1 | 2 | 3 | 4 |

I can synthesize information from four sources.

| 1 | 2 | 3 | 4 |

Think about what you learned. Fill in the bars. What helped you do your best?

# What I Learned

I can write an argumentative essay.

I can synthesize information from four sources.

1 > 2 > 3 > 4

## WRITE TO SOURCES

You will answer an argumentative writing prompt using sources and a rubric.

## ANALYZE THE RUBRIC

A rubric tells you what needs to be included in your writing.

**Purpose, Focus, and Organization**

Read the fourth bullet. What is a synonym for the word *logical*?

_____

_____

**Evidence and Elaboration**

Read the second bullet. What is the connection between evidence and the logical progression of ideas?

_____

_____

_____

_____

_____

# Argumentative Writing Rubric

### Purpose, Focus, and Organization • Score 4

- stays focused on the purpose, audience, and task
- makes a claim that clearly supports a perspective
- uses transitional strategies, such as words and phrases, to connect ideas
- **presents ideas in a logical progression, or order**
- begins with a strong introduction and ends with a strong conclusion

### Evidence and Elaboration • Score 4

- effectively supports the claim with logical reasons
- has strong examples of relevant evidence, or supporting details, from multiple sources
- uses elaborative techniques, such as examples, definitions, and quotations from sources
- expresses interesting ideas, clearly using precise language
- uses appropriate academic and domain-specific language
- uses different sentence structures

Turn to page 236 for the complete Argumentative Writing Rubric.

# Logical Progression

**Organize Ideas** When writers present evidence and reasons in an argumentative essay, they order the information in a logical way. The introduction contains the claim. The middle paragraphs support the claim with reasons and supporting evidence. The conclusion sums up the supporting information and restates the claim. Transition words can be used to connect ideas. Read the paragraphs below.

**Audience**

Read the two paragraphs in the box. Who do you think the audience is? What words helped you figure out the audience for these paragraphs?

> **Did you know that some students plant flowers to attract butterflies and help the environment?** Or that a five-year-old boy could help save the ocean? Good things happen when kids volunteer, and it's something that all of us at this school should do.
>
> To start with, there are some things we can do in our school. In Livingston, New Jersey, middle school students worked with community members to create a monarch-friendly butterfly garden.

In the first paragraph, the sentence introducing the claim about volunteering is highlighted. What evidence in the second paragraph gives a logical progression of that idea?

_____

_____

Reread the first paragraph. What do you think the third paragraph might be about?

_____

# WRITING

## ANALYZE THE STUDENT MODEL

**Paragraph 1**

**Underline** the claim. What is the purpose of Michael's essay?

_____

_____

_____

_____

**Paragraph 2**

**Circle** the sentence that helps to transition from butterfly gardens to vegetable gardens. How does Michael elaborate on his idea of a vegetable garden?

_____

_____

_____

_____

_____

_____

_____

Michael responded to the Writing Prompt: *Write an argumentative essay to present at a school assembly about whether or not kids should spend time volunteering.* Read Michael's essay below.

1    Did you know that some students plant flowers to attract butterflies and help the environment? Or that a five-year-old boy could help save the ocean? Good things happen when kids volunteer, and it's something that all of us at this school should do.

2    To start with, there are some things that we can do in our school. We could plant a butterfly or vegetable garden. In a middle school in Livingston, New Jersey, students worked with community members to create a monarch-friendly butterfly garden. Butterfly gardens support native plant habitats. Plus, the gardens are a fun way to be in nature and learn more about plants. Another good garden idea is to grow vegetables. The cafeteria could use some of the vegetables in our school lunches. We could also donate some of the produce to a local food bank. In the article "Food for Thought," a middle school in Orlando, Florida planted a vegetable garden. They sold the produce and donated the money to an animal shelter.

3    Volunteers, like the kids who planted the gardens, make a positive difference in the world. But according to the article "Public Service Volunteers," only about 27% of

Titus Group/Shutterstock

Americans volunteer. More volunteers are needed. There are all kinds of ways to help! Remember the five-year-old boy I mentioned? His name is Ryan. He is from Alabama and is helping to protect our oceans and sea animals. He started making things with sea animals on them and selling them when he was five to raise money. He donates the money he makes to the Ocean Conservancy. It's an organization that helps to protect our oceans. Ryan's example shows that even just one person can make a difference.

4    Surprisingly, not everyone agrees that kids should spend time volunteering. Some people think kids should just focus on school. In an editorial about kids volunteering, the writer said, "The only things I want my kids to worry about are school and having fun." I disagree. It is never too early for kids to start volunteering. My class last year had a bake sale to raise money for hurricane victims; we raised $450 and had fun. Best of all, we knew that we were helping others.

5    As you can see, spending time volunteering is a very good thing! It is a fun way to help others, and it teaches us that we can make a positive difference in the world. So let's all volunteer!

## ARGUMENTATIVE ESSAY

**Paragraph 1 and Paragraph 3**
Reread the first paragraph and the third paragraph. The highlighted text shows the logical progression of Michael's argument. What else is the highlighted sentence in paragraph 3 an example of?

_____

_____

**Paragraph 4**
Michael includes an opposing argument. **Draw a box** around the argument. How does Michael respond to the argument?

_____

_____

**Paragraph 5**
Reread the conclusion. **Underline** the idea that Michael restates from his introduction.

### Apply the Rubric

With a partner, use the rubric on page 86 to discuss why Michael scored a 4 on his essay.

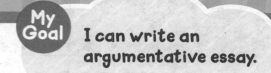

# Analyze the Prompt

## Writing Prompt

*Write an argumentative essay for a school bulletin board display about why the civil rights movement was needed.*

**Purpose, Audience, and Task** Reread the writing prompt. What is your purpose for writing? My purpose is to _____

_____

Who will your audience be? My audience will be _____

_____

What type of writing is the prompt asking for? _____

_____

**Set a Purpose for Reading Sources** For this response, you will use four sources. Three sources are on pages 91–93, and the fourth is "Keeping Freedom in the Family," on pages 216–219 in the **Literature Anthology**. Think about what you already know about civil rights. Then write what you would like to learn about the topic below.

_____

_____

_____

Read the following passage set.

# Civil Rights Pioneers

1      Harry T. and Harriette V. Moore were early civil rights activists in Florida in the early 1930s. At the time, there were no equal rights for African Americans. They wanted to change things. **In 1934, they started the first branch of the National Association for the Advancement of Colored People (NAACP) in Brevard County.** The NAACP was founded in 1909 to fight for equal rights for people of all races.

2      The Moores organized and wrote letters to protest unequal pay and segregated schools. **In 1945, they helped to start the Progressive Voters League.** They knew it was important for African Americans to vote. The organization registered over 100,000 African Americans throughout the state. Today, The Harry T. & Harriette V. Moore Cultural Complex in Brevard County honors this civil rights couple.

## Civil Rights Pioneers

**1909**
The NAACP was founded for equal rights for all.

**1934**
The first NAACP branch in Florida was started by the Moores.

**1945**
The Moores helped to start the Progressive Voters League.

---

## ARGUMENTATIVE ESSAY

### FIND TEXT EVIDENCE

**Paragraphs 1–2**
**Underline** the details that tell you why the NAACP was founded. Why did the Moores start a branch in Florida?

_____

_____

Read the highlighted sentences. What text structure is being used to present information in a logical order?

_____

_____

**Circle** the detail that tells you how many African American voters the organization helped to register.

**Timeline**
How many years was it between when the Moores started the Florida NAACP and the Progressive Voters League?

_____

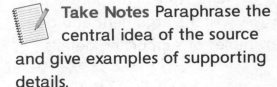 **Take Notes** Paraphrase the central idea of the source and give examples of supporting details.

## FIND TEXT EVIDENCE

**Paragraph 3**

What is the purpose of this essay?

_____

_____

_____

_____

**Paragraphs 4–5**

Read the highlighted sentences in each paragraph. **Circle** the transition words in each sentence. Why are these transition words important?

_____

_____

_____

**Underline** the sentence that tells you why Rosa Parks was arrested. **Draw a box** around the detail that tells you how the boycott affected the city buses.

**Take Notes** Paraphrase the writer's argument and give examples of supporting details.

**SOURCE 2**

# The Montgomery Bus Boycott

3     Boycotts—refusing to buy from or support a government agency—are peaceful protests. The Montgomery Bus Boycott shows how boycotts can bring about change.

4     On December 1, 1955, an African American woman named Rosa Parks took a stand. **At that time in Montgomery, Alabama, African Americans had to sit in segregated, or separate, sections at the back of buses and give up their seats if a white person needed one.** Parks wanted to change this. One day Parks was in her seat on the bus. More white people got on and the driver asked Parks and three others to give up their seats. Parks said no. As a result, the police arrested Parks.

5     Parks was the secretary of the Montgomery NAACP. She had always worked for equal rights for African Americans. Her arrest was the breaking point. Martin Luther King, Jr., a local minister, joined with others in calling all African Americans in Montgomery to boycott the city buses. The boycott planned for one day lasted a year. **Soon all of America was paying attention to these events.** In November 1956, the US Supreme Court ruled that states could not require segregation on buses.

6     The Montgomery Bus Boycott was the first large protest against segregation in the United States. Martin Luther King, Jr. became an important civil rights leader during that time. It was the beginning of many nonviolent protests demanding fair treatment under the law.

Don Cravens/The LIFE Images Collection/Getty Images

# FREEDOM SUMMER AND THE CIVIL RIGHTS MOVEMENT

7    It was the summer of 1964. The Student Nonviolent Coordinating Committee, or SNCC, was standing up for African American civil rights in remote parts of Mississippi. Boycotts that worked well in cities did not work well in rural places. However, the SNCC wanted to address the problems African Americans faced when they tried to vote.

8    Robert Moses, an SNCC activist, started the Mississippi Summer Project, also called Freedom Summer. Volunteers from the North came to Mississippi to help African Americans register to vote. They also created Freedom Schools for African American students. They wanted students to continue to seek and stand up for their rights after the summer ended.

9    About 17,000 African Americans tried to register to vote during those months. However, some local people objected, and registrars only accepted 1,600 of the applications. Tragically, volunteers were killed. Some local people who supported the movement were banned from stores or fired from their jobs. The local police did nothing.

10   Freedom Summer got the world's attention. It led to the passage of the Civil Rights Act of 1964 and, later, the Voting Rights Act of 1965. By 1969, it is estimated that the percentage of African Americans of voting age who were registered to vote had more than doubled because of these laws.

Library of Congress Prints and Photographs Division ILC-DIG-ppmsca-081021

## ARGUMENTATIVE ESSAY

**FIND TEXT EVIDENCE** 🔍

**Paragraph 8**
**Circle** the goals that the SNCC had for their civil rights campaign.

**Paragraph 9**
**Underline** the details about what happened when 17,000 African Americans tried to register to vote. What happened to some of the volunteers and local supporters?

_____

_____

_____

**Paragraph 10**
What was the positive outcome of Freedom Summer?

_____

_____

_____

_____

**Take Notes** Paraphrase the central idea of the source and give examples of supporting details.

## TAKE NOTES

Read the writing prompt below. Write your claim. Then use the four sources, your notes, and the graphic organizer to plan a response.

**Writing Prompt** *Write an argumentative essay for a school bulletin board display about why the civil rights movement was needed.*

### Synthesize Information

Review your notes from the four sources that you read about the civil rights movement. Think about what you know about the topic. Then discuss with a partner what the protests and marches achieved.

CHECK IN &gt; 1 &gt; 2 &gt; 3 &gt; 4 &gt;

# Plan: Organize Ideas

| | |
|---|---|
| **Introduction** (Make the claim) | The civil rights movement was needed because . . . |
| **Body** (List supporting reasons) | According to "Civil Rights Pioneers," . . . |
| | According to "The Montgomery Bus Boycott," African Americans were treated unfairly on buses in Montgomery, Alabama. |
| | |
| | |
| **Conclusion** (Summarize supporting information) | |

## Relevant Evidence
List relevant evidence from four sources

# Draft: Sentence Fluency

**Sentence Fluency** The term *sentence fluency* means "how words sound together within a sentence, and how sentences sound when read one after the other." Use transition words and simple and compound sentences to make your sentences more interesting. Remember that end punctuation also helps to vary your sentences. Read the paragraph below.

> Mary McLeod Bethune is my hero! In 1904, Bethune started her own school for African American girls in Daytona, Florida. At that time, schools were segregated, so most African American schools did not have the resources that white schools did. Bethune believed that everybody was entitled to a good education. As she famously said, "The whole world opened to me when I learned to read."

Use the above paragraph as a model to write a paragraph for your argumentative essay. Remember to experiment with longer and shorter sentence lengths.

_____

_____

_____

_____

 **Draft** Use your graphic organizer and paragraph to write your draft in your writer's notebook. Before you start writing, review the rubric on page 86.

### Grammar Connections

A simple sentence, or independent clause, shows a complete thought: *The bird sang.*

A compound sentence has two independent clauses that are usually connected with a coordinating conjunction and often with a comma: *The bird sang, and the dog barked.*

Make sure your simple and compound sentences have a subject and a verb to avoid any sentence fragments.

CHECK IN 1 2 3 4

# Revise: Peer Conferences

COLLABORATE

**Review a Draft** Listen actively to your partner. Take notes about what you liked and what was difficult to follow. Begin by telling what you liked. Use these sentence starters.

*The way you organized your argument helped me understand . . .*
*What did you mean by . . .*
*I think varying your sentences . . .*

After you give each other feedback, reflect on the peer conference. How can you use the guidance from your partner to help improve your writing?

_____

_____

_____

**Revision** Use the Revising Checklist to help you figure out what text you may need to move, elaborate on, or delete. After you finish writing your final draft, use the full rubric on pages 236–239 to score your essay.

### Revising Checklist

- ☐ Did I include enough reasons and evidence to support my claim?
- ☐ Did I present my ideas in a logical order?
- ☐ Did I use transitional strategies to show the connections between ideas?
- ☐ Did I vary my sentences?
- ☐ Did I check my spelling and punctuation?

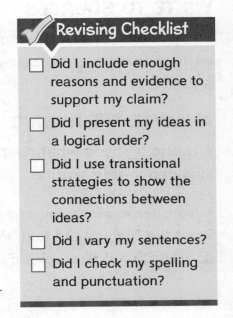

Next, you'll write an argumentative essay on a new topic.

| My Score | | | |
|---|---|---|---|
| Purpose, Focus, & Organization (4 pts) | Evidence & Elaboration (4 pts) | Conventions (2 pts) | Total (10 pts) |
| | | | |

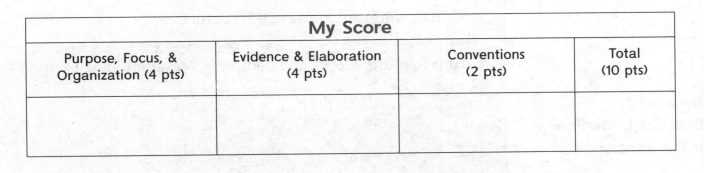

## WRITE TO SOURCES

You will answer an argumentative writing prompt using sources and a rubric.

## ANALYZE THE RUBRIC

A rubric tells you what needs to be included in your writing.

**Purpose, Focus, and Organization**
Read the highlighted text. What do transitional strategies connect?

_____

_____

_____

**Evidence and Elaboration**
Read the second bullet. Write an example of a phrase that you could use to introduce a source in a response.

_____

_____

**Evidence and Elaboration**
Read the fourth bullet. **Underline** an antonym for the word _unclear_.

# Argumentative Writing Rubric

### Purpose, Focus, and Organization • Score 4

- stays focused on the purpose, audience, and task
- makes a claim that clearly supports a perspective
- **uses transitional strategies, such as words and phrases, to connect ideas**
- presents ideas in a logical progression, or order
- begins with a strong introduction and ends with a strong conclusion

### Evidence and Elaboration • Score 4

- effectively supports the claim with logical reasons
- has strong examples of relevant evidence, or supporting details, from multiple sources
- uses elaborative techniques, such as examples, definitions, and quotations from sources
- expresses interesting ideas clearly using precise language
- uses appropriate academic and domain-specific language
- uses different sentence structures

Turn to page 236 for the complete Argumentative Writing Rubric.

# Transitional Strategies

**Transition Words** Effective writers use signal, or transition, words and phrases to help readers understand the relationships between ideas. Some common signal words and phrases used to link ideas are *and, in addition, also, but, so, with, because, finally, first, next, then, even, when,* and *therefore*. Read the paragraph below. Then revise it to add transition words that connect ideas.

**Task**

If your task is to write a comparison essay, some useful words that link ideas are *both, in contrast, but, although,* and *nevertheless*.

Some transition words that signal a cause-and-effect relationship are *as a result, because, since,* and *so*.

A waterwheel is a big wheel. It has paddles on the rim. The force of the water hits the paddles. The wheel turns. The wheel runs machinery linked to it. Ancient Egyptians used river currents to turn wheels. The ancient Greeks used power created by moving water. The Romans also used it.

_____

_____

_____

_____

_____

_____

_____

_____

## ANALYZE THE STUDENT MODEL

**Paragraph 1**

**Circle** the details that tell why Michelle is in favor of solar panels.

**Paragraphs 2-3**

Read the second paragraph. The transition words in paragraph 2 are highlighted. **Draw a box** around another example of a transition in paragraph 3.

What evidence does Michelle present in paragraph 2 to support her argument that solar energy can help save money?

_____

_____

_____

_____

**Paragraph 3**

**Underline** the details that support the idea that solar power helps the environment.

# Student Model: Argumentative Essay

Michelle responded to the Writing Prompt: *Write an editorial for the local town paper about whether solar panels should be put on the library and the elementary school.* Read Michelle's essay below.

**1**      What does New Mexico have plenty of? Sunshine! Solar power is free energy, and it's reliable. Best of all, it is pollution-free! I know that some people think that solar energy is more trouble than it's worth. They say that it's too expensive. However, putting solar panels on the roof of our local elementary school and library branch will save money. It will also help the environment.

**2**      **According to** the article "Sunshine Power in New Mexico," solar power makes a lot of sense in New Mexico. In 2020, New Mexico passed a solar tax credit. This credit makes it cheaper to install solar panels. Solar panels change sunlight into electricity. That electricity can run everything in a building or house. **And** if the solar panels generate extra electricity, the power company will pay to use that extra power.

**3**      Since the library and elementary school are both big, we could put a lot of solar panels on them. Silver City averages 295 days of sun a year. This means we will have plenty of energy. Using solar panels will also be good for the environment! Unlike oil or gas, solar energy doesn't produce carbon dioxide or air pollution. That's one of the reasons that my parents are thinking about putting ground-mounted solar panels in our yard.

4     Some people are concerned about the cost of solar energy. The article "Problems with Solar Power" says that "installing solar panels on a house is expensive. Experienced people need to do the installation." In addition, solar power can cost up to eleven times more than energy from other sources, like coal. It may take many years before people figure out ways to make the solar panels less expensive. However, there are also tax breaks that can help with the cost. Eventually, the system will pay for itself, but it may take up to ten years. I believe it's worth the cost because we need to think about the future of our planet.

5     My vote is for the city to invest in solar energy. After all, New Mexico ranks number one in peak sun hours in the United States. Over time, our city will save money. Future residents of our neighborhood will be grateful that we switched to solar power. The best part of the idea is that solar power is a renewable energy source. That is good for the environment!

Monkey Business Images/Shutterstock

**Paragraph 4**

**Underline** the central idea in paragraph 4.

**Circle** the evidence that Michelle presents to counter the argument that solar power is expensive. Does presenting a problem with solar power make Michelle's essay stronger? Why or why not?

_____
_____
_____
_____
_____
_____

**Paragraph 5**

**Draw a box** around the end punctuation that helps to emphasize Michelle's claim.

**Apply the Rubric**

With a partner, use the rubric on page 98 to discuss why Michelle scored a 4 on her essay.

My Goal **I can write an argumentative essay.**

## Analyze the Prompt

### Writing Prompt

*Write an argumentative essay for your class explaining why stricter protections are needed for Oregon's Willamette River Basin.*

**Purpose, Audience, and Task** Reread the writing prompt. What is your purpose for writing? My purpose is to _____

_____

Who will your audience be? My audience will be _____

_____

What type of writing is the prompt asking for? _____

_____

**Set a Purpose for Reading Sources** Asking questions about why stricter protections are needed for Oregon's Willamette River Basin will help you figure out your purpose for reading. It also helps you understand what you already know about the topic. Before you read the passage set, write a question here.

_____

_____

_____

Read the following passage set.

# A River in Danger

1    Recent changes to the Clean Water Act have stripped away the protections for some of the streams and wetlands near Oregon's Willamette River. The Willamette River is the thirteenth largest river by volume in the United States. Its nearby wetlands and waterways are all part of the same watershed as the river. A watershed is an area where water drains into one place.

2    Pollution of the Willamette has been a problem for a long time. One source for the Willamette River is Waldo Lake, one of the world's purest lakes. However, by the time the Willamette reaches the Columbia River, its waters contain pollutants. One issue is that rain and snowmelt in the watershed pick up pollutants like fertilizer, trash, and oil from cars. These eventually end up in the Willamette River.

3    In 1972, the Clean Water Act put limits on what could be dumped into the river. A 2015 revision of the act included protections for nearby waters that affect the river's water quality. However, in 2020, the Clean Water Act was changed again. Now many streams and wetlands are no longer protected.

4    The Willamette River is an important source of water in Oregon. Its waters are used to give life to crops on farms. People catch fish there. Several communities get their drinking water from the river. Strong protections are needed for the water near this important river.

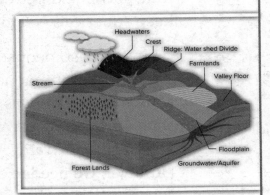

## ARGUMENTATIVE ESSAY

### FIND TEXT EVIDENCE

**Paragraph 1**
**Circle** the author's claim. What is a watershed?

_____

_____

_____

**Paragraph 2**
**Underline** the details that explain how the Williamette River becomes polluted.

**Paragraph 3**
What did the 2015 revision to the Clean Water Act change?

_____

_____

_____

**Paragraph 4**
**Draw a box** around the details that tell you why the Williamette River is important.

**Take Notes** Paraphrase the author's claim and give examples of supporting information.

# WRITING

## FIND TEXT EVIDENCE

**Paragraph 5**

What word describes what the DEQ believes making the changes to the act will do to the drinking water?

_____

**Paragraph 6**

**Underline** the words that tell you what the EPA says changing the act will allow.

**Paragraph 7**

What did one Oklahoma senator say the change would do?

_____

**Paragraph 8**

**Circle** the details that tell you what the writer of the article says happens when pipelines are not constructed.

📝 **Take Notes** Paraphrase the central idea of "Balancing Conservation and Energy Needs" and give examples of supporting details.

**SOURCE 2**

# Balancing Conservation and Energy Needs

**(To the editor of _Oregon News_)**

5    Recently, the Oregon Department of Environmental Quality, or DEQ, issued a statement. They criticized the 2020 changes to the Clean Water Act. The DEQ said that making these changes "under the guise of 'efficiency' will endanger our drinking water . . . and more."

6    However, increasing efficiency is important. The Environmental Protection Agency, or EPA, argues that the old act slowed things down too much. Changing the act allows people to more quickly grow our infrastructure. Infrastructure involves facilities that support modern life. Examples include roads, buildings, and power supplies.

7    Many lawmakers across the country agree the reforms were needed. An Oklahoma senator said that the change will allow water quality reviews to focus on water alone. He pointed out that those reviews should not "block pipelines and needed infrastructure projects." Energy pipelines transport liquid petroleum and natural gas. These fossil fuels keep America's economy going.

8    In the past, people have used the Clean Water Act as a way of preventing new pipelines from being constructed. This was slowing down our state's growth. Our water is important, and the Clean Water Act still protects it. However, we need to address _both_ conservation and energy needs. Each is important to Oregon's future.

Steve Oehlenschlager/123RF

# A Winter Refuge for Geese

9    If you visit the William L. Finley National Wildlife Refuge in the fall, you're likely to hear a lot of honking! That honking isn't cars. It comes from the more than 250,000 geese that spend the winter in the Willamette Valley of Oregon.

10    The Willamette Valley surrounds the Willamette River in Oregon. Its wetlands were home to many migrating birds. Since the 1800s, the valley's human population has grown very large. Communities drained wetland areas. The dusky goose, a type of Canada goose, was disappearing because of habitat loss. By the 1960s, conservationists knew something needed to be done. They decided to create wildlife refuges.

11    The William L. Finley National Wildlife Refuge is one of three refuges protecting valuable valley wetlands. To make a welcoming winter home for geese, the refuge works with local farmers who plant special grass crops. The farmers benefit by harvesting the grasses as hay for their livestock. Returning geese benefit as they eat the grasses' new fall growth. Some Oregon groups even give funds to valley farmers to help them restore wetlands on the edges of cropland. This creates even more overwintering places for the geese.

12    The valley's wetlands still face challenges. Pollution from human activities affects the water quality in the area. There is pressure to build infrastructure projects in wild places. Oregon lawmakers need to continue to protect the wetlands. By doing this, they protect the animals that make them their home.

Peter K. Ziminski/Shutterstock

## FIND TEXT EVIDENCE

**Paragraph 10**
**Circle** the reason why communities drained wetland areas.

**Paragraph 11**
**Underline** how the special grass crops benefit farmers and geese. What do some groups do that helps even more?

_____

_____

_____

**Paragraph 12**
What challenges do the wetlands still face?

_____

_____

_____

_____

**Take Notes** Paraphrase the impact that humans have had on waterways and what is being done to fix it.

# WRITING

**My Goal** I can synthesize information from three sources.

## TAKE NOTES

Read the writing prompt below. Write your claim. Then use the three sources, your notes, and the graphic organizer to plan a response.

**Writing Prompt** *Write an argumentative essay for your class explaining why stricter protections are needed for Oregon's Willamette River Basin.*

 Synthesize Information

Review the evidence recorded from each source. What are the top three reasons that protections are needed in Oregon's Williamette River Basin? Discuss your ideas with a partner.

CHECK IN  1 ⟩ 2 ⟩ 3 ⟩ 4 ⟩

# Plan: Organize Ideas

| Introduction (Make the claim) | Stricter protections are needed for Oregon's Willamette River Basin. |
|---|---|
| **Body** (List supporting reasons) | According to "A River in Danger," . . . |
| | |
| | |
| **Conclusion** (Summarize supporting information) | |

Valentain Jevee/Shutterstock

## Relevant Evidence

List relevant evidence from three sources

| | | |
|---|---|---|
| | | |
| | | |
| | | |

# Draft: Domain-Specific Vocabulary

**Content-Area Words** Writers use domain-specific vocabulary when they are writing about a science, social studies, or other content-area topic. When you use domain-specific terms to write about a topic, readers will have a better understanding of the topic. However, remember your audience. It may be necessary to include some definitions for domain-specific vocabulary if your audience is not familiar with the topic.

Read the sentences below. Then rewrite them using domain-specific vocabulary to make the writing clearer and more precise.

> People who grow things that we eat want to keep bugs off the stuff they grow. Sometimes they spray things on the stuff they grow. If the stuff they spray gets into a lake, it can do bad things to all the living things in the lake.

_____

_____

_____

_____

_____

**Draft** Use your graphic organizer to write your draft in your writer's notebook. Before you start writing, review the rubric on page 98. Remember to use transition words and domain-specific vocabulary.

### Grammar Connections

Varying sentences will make your essay more interesting to read. Ask a question at the beginning of a paragraph: *Why is water important?*

Try adding an exclamation mark: *People need water to survive!*

Or try beginning a sentence with a verb: *Swimming in the ocean . . .*

CHECK IN  1  2  3  4

MSPT/Shutterstock

# Revise: Peer Conferences

COLLABORATE

**Review a Draft** Listen actively to your partner. Take notes about what you liked and what was difficult to follow. Begin by telling what you liked. Use these sentence starters.

*Your transitional words helped me understand . . .*
*What did you mean by . . .*
*I think adding more domain-specific words . . .*

After you give each other feedback, reflect on the peer conference. How can you use the guidance from your partner to help improve your writing?

_____

_____

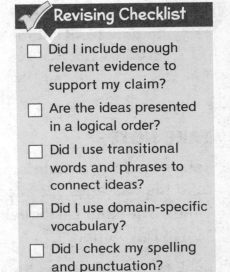

Turn to page 85. Fill in the bars to show what you learned.

## Revising Checklist

- [ ] Did I include enough relevant evidence to support my claim?
- [ ] Are the ideas presented in a logical order?
- [ ] Did I use transitional words and phrases to connect ideas?
- [ ] Did I use domain-specific vocabulary?
- [ ] Did I check my spelling and punctuation?

**Revision** Use the Revising Checklist to help you figure out what text you may need to move, elaborate on, or delete. After you finish writing your final draft, use the full rubric on pages 236–239 to score your essay.

| My Score | | | |
|---|---|---|---|
| Purpose, Focus, & Organization (4 pts) | Evidence & Elaboration (4 pts) | Conventions (2 pts) | Total (10 pts) |
| | | | |

## TAKE NOTES

Take notes and annotate as you read the passages "Challenging Times: The 1886 Earthquake" and "Earth Day Action."

Look for the answer to the question: *What improvements did people make after major disasters?*

PASSAGE 1 · EXPOSITORY TEXT

# CHALLENGING TIMES: THE 1886 EARTHQUAKE

By 1886, Charleston, South Carolina, had suffered through difficult times. The Great Fire of 1861, the Civil War, and Reconstruction, the period after the war, had done much damage to the city. A major hurricane hit Charleston in 1885, destroying parts of the city's seawall and flooding streets. But no one expected what would come next.

August 31, 1886, was a hot summer day. At 9:50 p.m., the earth beneath the city suddenly began to shake. Streets rose and fell like waves, throwing buildings and homes aside. A train fell off its tracks.

The earthquake lasted only about a minute, but that short period was devastating. It was the biggest earthquake ever to strike the East Coast of the United States. People felt tremors as far north as Canada and as far south as Cuba.

Because a large earthquake was so unexpected, the city was unprepared. Buildings had not been constructed to withstand an earthquake. Initially, people rushed in terror out of buildings, and most stayed outside the rest of the night. Aftershocks shook the ground. Many city buildings had crumbled or cracked. The quake destroyed telegraph lines and railroads, making it hard to communicate. At least 86 people died—many because of lack of fresh water and other bad conditions.

Photograph by J.K. Hillers, USGS

The earthquake became the basis of a large and important scientific study. Scientists had gathered data on the seismic waves that occurred during the earthquake. This helped them develop a new method for estimating the size and location of an earthquake. Throughout the country, scientists began to use this new method. It helped people learn more about earthquakes and why they occur.

**EXPOSITORY TEXT**

# EARTH DAY ACTION

Each year, more than 1 billion people take part in Earth Day activities throughout the world. The very first Earth Day took place in 1970. A US senator from Wisconsin saw the impact an oil spill had on the coast of California. He decided to take action. He worked to establish a day each year when people set aside time to learn about and be inspired to protect the environment. That day is April 22. Here are some ideas for how you can take action on Earth Day—or any day of the year—to help protect Earth.

**Take a Listening Walk** Go on a ten-minute, talk-free walk. Tune in to the natural sounds around you. Think about the sounds you hear, such as leaves rustling, birds chirping, or insects buzzing. At the end of your walk, talk about the different sounds you heard.

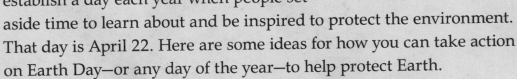

(c) Alistair Berg/DigitalVision/Getty Images; (b) MarBom/Shutterstock

## TAKE NOTES

_____

_____

_____

_____

_____

_____

_____

_____

_____

_____

_____

_____

_____

_____

_____

_____

_____

_____

_____

_____

## TAKE NOTES

_____

_____

_____

_____

_____

_____

_____

_____

_____

_____

_____

_____

_____

_____

_____

_____

_____

_____

_____

**Pick Up Litter Near Your School** Pick an area near your school to clean up. Take a picture of the area before you start. Be sure to wear gloves and carry a container for the litter. As you pick up litter, keep track of what you find and where. Take a picture of the cleaned-up area. Then analyze the information about what you found and where you found it. Use your analysis to brainstorm solutions about how to stop the litter.

**Make a Pledge** Decide on one step you will take to protect the environment. Will you always turn off water while you brush your teeth? Will you learn how composting can reduce waste? Write your pledge down and share it with your classmates.

**Make Signs for School or Home** Create colorful signs to remind people how they can help protect Earth and its resources. (Don't forget to turn off the light! Recycle or reuse! Recycle old electronic devices!) Post them in your classroom or school.

## COMPARE THE PASSAGES

Create a Venn diagram like the one below. Use it to write about how the information in "Challenging Times: The 1886 Earthquake" and "Earth Day Action" is alike and different.

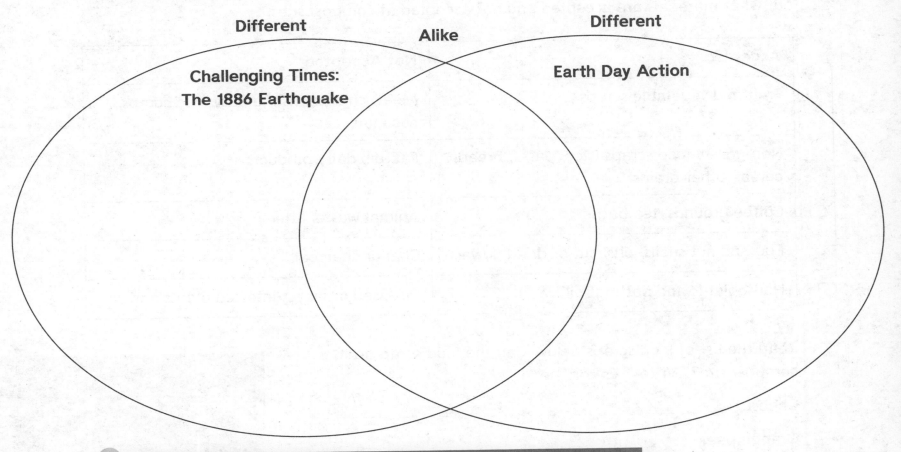

**Different**          **Alike**          **Different**

**Challenging Times:
The 1886 Earthquake**          **Earth Day Action**

### Synthesize Information

Think about both texts. What inspires people to make changes after environmental disasters? Write your response in your reader's notebook.

## COMPOST FOOD SCRAPS AND PLANTS

Many towns and cities have compost sites where you can bring your food scraps and plants. The compost is used to improve the quality of soil for trees, gardens, farms, and much more. Look at the chart below to find out what materials are accepted and not accepted at compost sites.

| Accepted | Not Accepted |
| --- | --- |
| Fruit and vegetable scraps | Meat, chicken, fish, greasy food scraps, coconuts |
| Non-greasy food scraps (rice, pasta, bread, cereal, other grains) | Fat, oil, dairy products |
| Coffee grounds, tea bags | Animal waste, litter |
| Egg and nut shells, pits, cut or dried flowers | Coal or charcoal |
| Houseplants and potting soil | Diseased or insect-infested plants and soil |

Read the list of food scraps below. Can the food scrap go to a compost site? Write "yes" or "no."

Cheese _____

Orange peel _____

Peach pit _____

Chicken bones _____

Peanut shells _____

## WRITE A SPEECH

Volunteers hoping to make a change in their community often have to speak about their project to government leaders or to people in their community. Choose a topic from one of the passages you read on pages 110-112 to write a speech about. Your speech should be brief—no more than two minutes long. In your speech, be sure to do the following.

• Introduce yourself and the state where your community is located.
• Clearly describe the focus of the project.
• Share some reasons why you think the project is important.
• Close by thanking your listeners.

Introduction: _____

Project focus: _____

_____

Reasons for the project: _____

_____

_____

Closing: _____

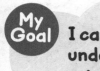

**My Goal** I can read and understand science texts.

## TAKE NOTES

Take notes and annotate as you read the passages "Flowering and Nonflowering Plants" and "Seasonal Changes."

Look for the answer to the question: *How do different plants change as they grow?*

_____

_____

_____

_____

_____

_____

_____

_____

_____

_____

_____

PASSAGE 1

EXPOSITORY TEXT

# FLOWERING AND NONFLOWERING PLANTS

Many plants you see every day, such as grasses and trees, are seed plants. Seed plants are classified by where they store their seeds.

**Flowering seed plants** bear fruit. Seeds are stored in the fruit, which protects the seeds. Study the life cycle of the orange plant below. Orange seeds are planted in soil. With the proper conditions, such as the right amount of sunlight, water, and nutrients, the seeds will sprout. Then the seeds will grow into a seedling, or young tree, with stems, roots, and leaves. As the orange tree continues to grow, flowers will blossom. Eventually the mature plant will produce oranges. The seeds in the oranges can continue the life cycle and produce more orange trees.

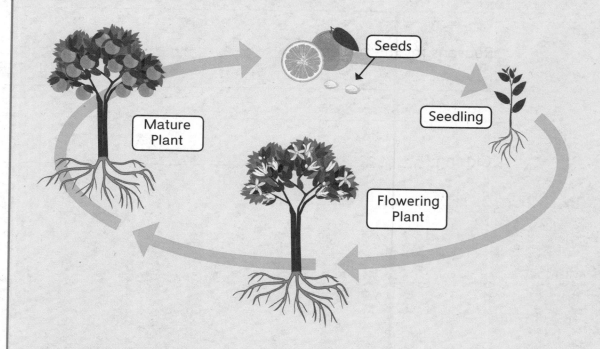

Mature Plant

Seeds

Seedling

Flowering Plant

Kazakova Maryia/Shutterstock

Pine trees, or conifers, are **nonflowering seed plants**. They do not have flowers or fruits. Instead, they have male and female pinecones. The male pinecones produce a yellow powder called "pollen." Wind or insects can carry the pollen from male pinecones to female pinecones. When the pollen grains from a male pinecone land on a female pinecone, seeds will develop, or fertilize, in the pinecone. When pinecones fall to the ground, the pine tree life cycle can start again.

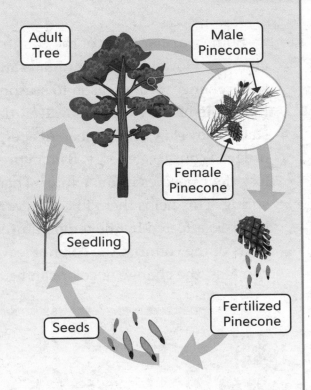

Adult Tree

Male Pinecone

Female Pinecone

Seedling

Fertilized Pinecone

Seeds

**PASSAGE 2**

EXPOSITORY TEXT

# Seasonal Changes

In most of the United States, the fall months mean tree leaves change color from green to orange, red, and yellow. Apples ripen on apple trees and pumpkins ripen in the fields. The air becomes cold and crisp almost overnight. Winter comes a few months later, bringing icy winds and snow. Trees and plants are in a dormant state (inactive or resting), conserving water and food during the cold months. Some animals hibernate, sleeping through the winter. During spring, the ground begins to warm up and the spring rains help the daffodils and tulips bloom. Animals wake from hibernation. Then come the hot, humid days of summer.

**TAKE NOTES**

## TAKE NOTES

_____

_____

_____

_____

_____

_____

_____

_____

_____

_____

_____

_____

_____

_____

_____

_____

Some warmer parts of the country do not have dramatic seasonal changes. However, some animals and plants in these areas go through some changes from season to season. Black bears in Florida do not hibernate in the winter. However, they do go into what is called a torpor state. They slow down, sleep deeper, and become much less active in order to conserve energy. Bald cypress trees, found in warmer climates, lose their needles in the winter. Then they grow new needles in the spring. This helps them to conserve water and food. Even the color of leaves is affected by the temperatures of the seasons. In some warmer parts of the country, the color of leaves changes very little. In cooler climates, the change of color can be quite dramatic.

**Autumn in Florida**

**Autumn in Vermont**

(t) jaimie tuchman/Shutterstock; (b) imagebroker/Alamy Stock Photo

## COMPARE THE PASSAGES

Review your notes from both passages. Then create a Venn diagram like the one below. Use your notes and the diagram to record how the information in the two passages is alike and different.

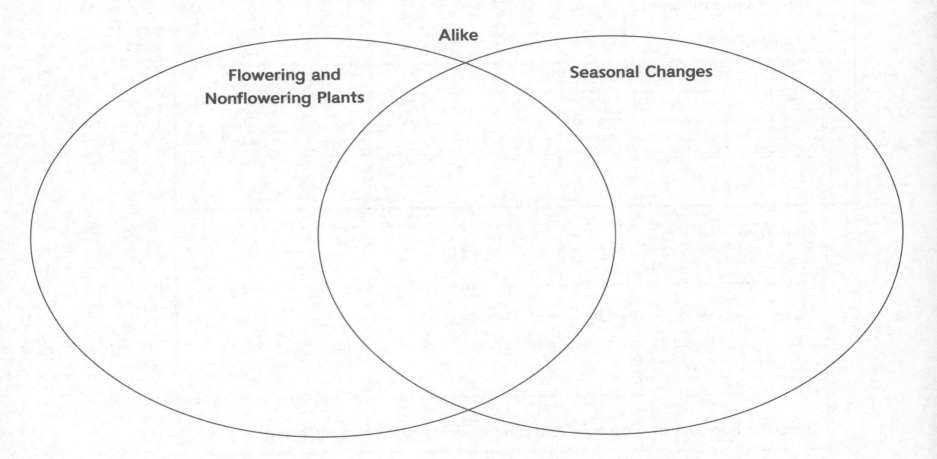

Alike

Flowering and
Nonflowering Plants

Seasonal Changes

**Synthesize Information**

Think about both texts. What affects the growth of plants and why? Write your response in your reader's notebook.

CHECK IN  1  2  3  4

## COMPARE AND CONTRAST FLOWERING AND NONFLOWERING PLANTS

A botanical garden needs signs to identify seed plants. The orange trees and pine trees need signs. Write a sign to identify whether the plant is a flowering or nonflowering plant and describe its life cycle. Then describe how the plants are alike and different.

**Orange Tree**

_____

_____

_____

_____

**Pine Tree**

_____

_____

_____

_____

**Describe how the orange tree and pine tree are alike and different.**

_____

_____

_____

# Reflect on Your Learning

**Talk About It** Reflect on what you learned in this unit. Then talk with a partner about how you did.

I am really proud of how I can _____

_____

_____

_____

Something I need to work more on is _____

_____

_____

_____

_____

 **My Goal** Set a goal for Unit 4. In your reader's notebook, write about what you can do to get there.

Share a goal you have with a partner.

# Build Knowledge

# Build Vocabulary

Write new words you learned about our government. Draw lines and circles for the words you write.

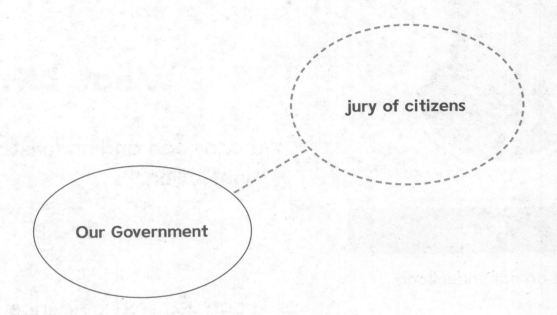

jury of citizens

Our Government

Go online to **my.mheducation.com** and read the "Vote for Me" Blast. Think about what you know about government and voting. Why is voting important? Then blast back your response.

Think about what you already know. Fill in the bars. This will be a good start.

# What I Know Now

### Key

| | |
|---|---|
| **1** = | I do not understand. |
| **2** = | I understand but need more practice. |
| **3** = | I understand. |
| **4** = | I understand and can teach someone. |

I can read and understand narrative nonfiction.

1 > 2 > 3 > 4

I can use text evidence to respond to narrative nonfiction.

1 > 2 > 3 > 4

I know why we need government.

1 > 2 > 3 > 4

 **STOP** You will come back to the next page later.

> Think about what you learned. Fill in the bars. What are you getting better at?

# What I Learned

I can read and understand narrative nonfiction.

1  2  3  4

I can use text evidence to respond to narrative nonfiction.

1  2  3  4

I know why we need government.

1  2  3  4

**My Goal** I can read and understand narrative nonfiction.

## TAKE NOTES

As you read, make note of interesting words and important information.

_____

_____

_____

_____

_____

_____

_____

_____

_____

_____

_____

_____

_____

# A WORLD WITHOUT RULES

## Essential Question

**?**

**Why do we need government?**

Read how government and laws help to protect us every day.

You may sometimes wonder if rules were made to keep you from having fun and to tell you what to do. But what if we had no rules at all? Nobody would tell you what to do ever again! Sounds great, right? Well, let's see what it's like to inhabit a world without rules. You just might change your mind!

## A Strange Morning

Let's start at home. Your alarm clock goes off. Why hurry? Without rules, you don't have to go to school. **Eventually** you wander downstairs and find your little brother eating cookies in the kitchen. Since there are no rules, you can have cookies for breakfast! But you wonder if you should have something sensible, like a bowl of cereal. You reach a **compromise (KOM•pru•mize)** and crumble the cookies over your cereal. In this new world, you will not have to brush your teeth anymore. No one will report you. Of course, the next time you see the dentist, you may have a cavity.

## A Community in Confusion

Now, you step outside. You decide to go to the playground because there's no law saying you have to go to school. No crossing guard stands at the corner to help you across the street. Without traffic laws, cars zip by at an alarming speed, honking at each other, and there is not a police officer in sight. There is no safe alternate way to cross the street. Besides, once you see the playground, you may decide it is not worth the risk of getting hit by a car. Broken swings dangle from rusty chains. Trash cans overflow with plastic bottles, snack wrappers, and paper bags. A huge tree branch lies across the slide. As a result of all city, state, and federal services being gone, nobody is in charge of taking care of the playground.

## FIND TEXT EVIDENCE

### Read

**Paragraphs 1–3**

### Cause and Effect

**Underline** the sentence in paragraph 1 that tells what the effect would be if we had no rules.
**Draw a box** around the words in paragraph 3 that tell what causes cars to zip by at an alarming speed.

### Ask and Answer Questions

What happens to a playground with no city, state, and federal services?

_____

_____

_____

_____

### Reread

## Author's Craft

How does the author's use of cause-and-effect text structure help you understand what would happen without rules?

## FIND TEXT EVIDENCE

**Read**

### Paragraphs 1-2

### Cause and Effect

**Circle** the words that tell you why you would not find a place to play soccer.

What is the effect of not having an army?

_____

_____

_____

### Paragraphs 3-4

### Headings

Why is "Back to Reality" a good heading for this section?

_____

_____

**Reread**

### Author's Craft

How does the author use headings to organize information?

Now think about trying to do all the other things you love. Want to go to the beach? The lifeguards will not be there to keep you safe. Want to play soccer in the park? Your state and local governments are not around to maintain the parks, so you'll never find a place to play. Feel like eating lunch outside? As a result of pollution, the air quality is so bad that you will probably have to wear a gas mask every day.

Have you ever thought about our country being invaded by another country? Remember, the government runs the army. Without the government, there is no army to protect us if another country decided to take over our country.

## Back to Reality

Thankfully, that **version** of our world isn't real. We live in a **democracy** (di•MOK•ruh•see) where we have the **privilege** (PRIV•uh•lij) of voting for the people whom we want to run the country. Our elected government passes **legislation** (lej•is•LAY•shuhn), or laws, meant to help and protect us. If the country outgrows an old law, then the government can pass **amendments** to the law. Community workers such as crossing guards, police officers, and lifeguards all work to keep you safe, while government agencies such as the Environmental Protection Agency have made a **commitment** to inspect the air and water for pollution. And don't forget the armed forces, which were created to protect our nation.

Our government and laws were designed to keep you safe and ensure that you are treated as fairly as everyone else. Without them, the world would be a different place.

**Summarize**

Use your notes and the headings to summarize the central idea and relevant details of "A World Without Rules."

## FIND TEXT EVIDENCE 🔍

**Read**

**Paragraphs 3-4**

### Pronunciations

**Draw a box** around the words that have pronunciations. Which of these words has the fewest syllables?

### Latin Roots

The Latin root *commun* means "together." **Underline** the word that contains the root. Write the word.

### Evaluate Information

Use the information in the text to tell why government agencies are important.

**Reread**

### Author's Craft

How does the author use reasons and evidence to show that we need rules?

# Vocabulary

**Use the example sentences to talk with a partner about each word. Then answer the questions.**

**amendments**

We made **amendments**, or changes, to the class rules.

Why do we need amendments?

_____

_____

**commitment**

I made a **commitment** to babysit for my little brother today.

What is a commitment you have made?

_____

_____

**compromise**

Sam and his dad agreed to **compromise** on when Sam should walk the dog.

Describe a time when you had to compromise.

_____

_____

**democracy**

In a **democracy**, the government is run by the people.

Why is voting an important right in a democracy?

_____

_____

**eventually**

The rain **eventually** stopped and the sun came out.

What job do you eventually want to have?

_____

_____

**Build Your Word List** Choose one of the interesting words you noted on page 126. Use a print or digital dictionary to look up the word's meaning. Then review how many syllables the word has and how it is pronounced.

**legislation**

Congress passes **legislation** to protect and help citizens.

Why might we need new legislation?

_____

_____

**privilege**

I had the **privilege** of running for class president.

What is a privilege you wish you had?

_____

_____

_____

**version**

I like the old **version** of this movie better than the new one.

What are some things that have different versions?

_____

_____

_____

## Latin Roots

Knowing Latin roots can help you figure out the meanings of unfamiliar words. Look for these Latin roots as you reread "A World Without Rules."

| | |
|---|---|
| *dent* = tooth | *port* = carry |
| *spect* = look | *commun* = together |

### 🔍 FIND TEXT EVIDENCE

*In the third paragraph on page 127, I see the word* alternate. *The Latin root* alter *means "other." This will help me figure out what* alternate *means.*

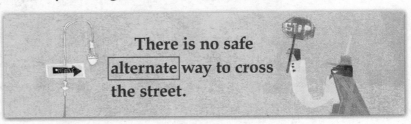

There is no safe alternate way to cross the street.

**Your Turn** Use Latin roots and context clues to figure out the meanings of these words.

**report,** page 127 _____

_____

**dentist,** page 127 _____

_____

**inspect,** page 128 _____

CHECK IN  1  2  3  4

# Ask and Answer Questions

As you read, you may come across new facts and ideas. Stop and ask yourself questions to help you understand and remember the information. Then read the text closely to find the answers.

 **FIND TEXT EVIDENCE**

When you first read the "Back to Reality" section in "A World Without Rules," you might have asked yourself what role the Environmental Protection Agency has in keeping people safe.

Page 128

> Community workers such as crossing guards, police officers, and lifeguards all work to keep you safe, while government agencies such as the Environmental Protection Agency have made a **commitment** to inspect the air and water for pollution.

*As I read on, I found the answer to my question. The Environmental Protection Agency's role is to inspect our air and water and make sure that they are clean.*

 **Your Turn** Read "Back to Reality" and ask a question about government. Find the answer and write it here.

_____

_____

_____

## Quick Tip

As you read a paragraph, underline any ideas on the topic that are not clear to you. Then ask yourself a question about the information you don't understand. Read on to find the answer.

CHECK IN  1  2  3  4

# Headings and Pronunciations

"A World Without Rules" is narrative nonfiction.

Narrative nonfiction

- tells a factual story in an interesting way
- may express the author's opinion about the subject
- presents facts and may include text features

## 🔍 FIND TEXT EVIDENCE

*"A World Without Rules" is narrative nonfiction. The author describes a situation and includes text features. The author also expresses an opinion and supports it with facts and examples.*

**Quick Tip**

Writers use word pronunciations to help the reader sound out unfamiliar words. A pronunciation will show how many syllables a word has and how the syllable should be stressed. How can you use pronunciations in your own nonfiction writing?

**Page 127**

You may sometimes wonder if rules were made to keep you from having fun and to tell you what to do. But what if we had no rules at all? Nobody would tell you what to do ever again! Sounds great, right? Well, let's see what it's like to inhabit a world without rules. You just might change your mind!

**A Strange Morning**

Let's start at home. Your alarm clock goes off. Why hurry? Without rules, you don't have to go to school. **Eventually** you wander downstairs and find your little brother eating cookies in the kitchen. Since there are no rules, you can have cookies for breakfast! But you wonder if you should have something sensible, like a bowl of cereal. You reach a **compromise (KOM·pru·mize)** and crumble the cookies over your cereal. In this new world, you will not have to brush your teeth anymore. No one will report you. Of course, the next time you see the dentist, you may have a cavity.

**A Community in Confusion**

Now, you step outside. You decide to go to the playground because there's no law saying you have to go to school. No crossing guard stands at the corner to help you across the street. Without traffic laws, cars zip by at an alarming speed, honking at each other, and there is not a police officer in sight. There is no safe alternate way to cross the street. Besides, once you see the playground, you may decide it is not worth the risk of getting hit by a car. Broken swings dangle from rusty chains. Trash cans overflow with plastic bottles, snack wrappers, and paper bags. A huge tree branch lies across the slide. As a result of all city, state, and federal services being gone, nobody is in charge of taking care of the playground.

**Headings** Headings tell you what the section is mostly about.

**Pronunciations** Pronunciations show how to sound out unfamiliar words.

**Your Turn** How does the author use headings to keep the reader interested?

_____

_____

_____

CHECK IN  1  2  3  4

# Cause and Effect

Authors use text structure to organize the information in a nonfiction text. **Cause and effect** is one kind of text structure. A cause is why something happens. An effect is what happens. Signal words such as *because, so, since,* and *as a result* can help you identify cause-and-effect relationships.

 **FIND TEXT EVIDENCE**

*When I reread the section "A Strange Morning" on page 127, I will look for causes and effects. I will also look for signal words.*

| Cause | → | Effect |
|---|---|---|
| Without rules | → | You don't have to go to school. |
| Without rules | → | You can have cookies for breakfast. |
| You don't have to brush your teeth. | → | You may get a cavity. |

**Your Turn** Reread the section "A Community in Confusion" on pages 127-128. Identify the causes and effects. List them in the graphic organizer on page 135.

CHECK IN  1  2  3  4

| Cause | → | Effect |
|---|---|---|
| | → | |
| | → | |
| | → | |
| | → | |

My Goal: I can use text evidence to respond to narrative nonfiction.

# Respond to Reading

Discuss the prompt below. Use your notes and text evidence to support your ideas.

Do you agree with the author that laws and government are important?

_____

_____

_____

_____

_____

_____

_____

_____

_____

_____

_____

_____

_____

_____

### Quick Tip

Use these sentence starters to discuss the text and organize your ideas.

- *I agree/disagree that . . .*
- *I think this because . . .*
- *One example the author uses is . . .*

### Grammar Connections

As you write your response, use transitions—words or phrases that link ideas together. Transitions form a bridge to take readers from one idea to the next. Here are some examples of transitions:

*for example, also, finally, generally, consequently, in the first place, in other words*

Remember, transitions that start a sentence are followed by a comma.

CHECK IN 》 1 》 2 》 3 》 4 》

# Government

COLLABORATE

It's important to understand the structure of your local government and how it functions. Follow the research process to create a slideshow about the different parts of government in your community, and the roles and responsibilities of each part. Work with a partner or group.

**Step 1** **Set a Goal** List questions you want your research to answer about how government in your community is organized.

**Step 2** **Identify Sources** Use books and websites to find information about what each part of your local government does.

**Step 3** **Find and Record Information** When reading sources, skimming and scanning will help. *Skim* means to read text quickly by reading the title, the headings, and the first sentence of each paragraph. *Scan* means to search for specific information in a text quickly. Take notes that answer your questions from Step 1. Remember to also look for images and sounds to use in your slideshow.

**Step 4** **Organize and Synthesize Information** Organize your notes and images. Be sure to include information that shows how your local government is organized, and the roles and responsibilities of each part.

**Step 5** **Create and Present** Create your slideshow. Think of how you will present it to your class.

**AIR QUALITY MEETING**

Concerned citizens are meeting this week to discuss how to improve air quality in our city.

**MAKE YOUR VOICE HEARD**

Do your part for clean air in the community. Join your fellow citizens at 8 p.m. on Thursday at the Town Hall. Mayor Jane Hamilton and many city council members are expected to speak.

Scan for the name of the mayor in the meeting notice. Write it here.

_____

CHECK IN ⟩ 1 ⟩ 2 ⟩ 3 ⟩ 4

# See How They Run

*Literature Anthology:*
*pages 270–281*

**?** **How does the author help you understand what the Founding Fathers did?**

**Talk About It** Reread page 273 of the **Literature Anthology**. Turn and talk to your partner about how George Washington and the Founding Fathers created our American government.

**Cite Text Evidence** What examples show how the Founding Fathers used ideas from Greek and Roman governments? Write text evidence in the chart.

**Synthesize Information**

Remember, when you synthesize information, you combine information to create a new understanding.

What were the differences between Roman and Greek governments? What were the similarities?

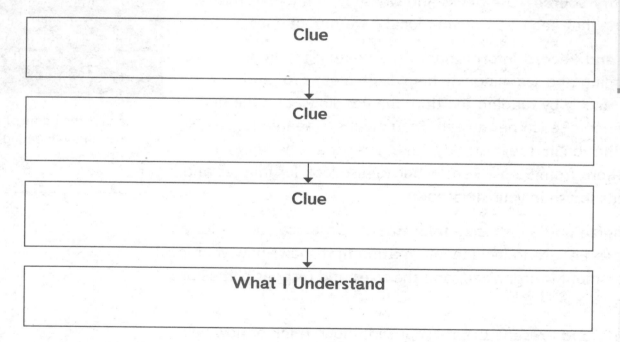

| Clue |
| --- |
|  |

↓

| Clue |
| --- |
|  |

↓

| Clue |
| --- |
|  |

↓

| What I Understand |
| --- |
|  |

**Write** The author helps me understand what the Founding Fathers did by

_____

_____

**?** **Why does the author include Benjamin Franklin's quote in the sidebar?**

**Talk About It** Reread the sidebar on page 274 of the **Literature Anthology**. Turn and talk with a partner about what Benjamin Franklin said.

**Cite Text Evidence** What words and phrases help you understand Benjamin Franklin's message? Write text evidence in the chart.

| Text Evidence | Author's Purpose |
|---|---|
| | |
| | |
| | |

**Write** The author includes Ben Franklin's quote to _____

_____

_____

### Quick Tip

Use these sentence starters when you talk about what Benjamin Franklin said.

- *Benjamin Franklin said that government needs its citizens to . . .*
- *This author uses this quote to show . . .*

### Make Inferences

Authors do not tell readers everything about the events or characters in a text. They give clues so readers can make inferences. To make an inference, look for clues in the text and use what you already know. Sidebars have added details that connect to the main text. What inference can you make about Benjamin Franklin based on the sidebar and the first sentence in the main text on page 274?

**CHECK IN** 1 2 3 4

**?** **Why does the author give specific, real-life examples of kids as leaders?**

**Quick Tip**

When you reread, look for specific details the author presents about kids becoming leaders.

**Talk About It** Reread page 279 of the **Literature Anthology**. Turn to your partner and talk about how Shadia Wood helped her community.

**Cite Text Evidence** What words and phrases show what Shadia did to help her community? Write text evidence in the chart.

| What Shadia Did | How It Helped | Author's Purpose |
|---|---|---|
| | | |

**Write** The author gives real-life examples of kids as leaders to

_____

_____

_____

CHECK IN  1  2  3  4

nito/Shutterstock.com

# Respond to Reading

Discuss the prompt below. Use your notes and text evidence to support your ideas.

Why is it important for people to participate in government?

_____

_____

_____

_____

_____

_____

_____

_____

_____

_____

_____

_____

_____

**Quick Tip**

Use these sentence starters to discuss the prompt and organize your ideas.

- *It is important to participate in government because . . .*

- *One way to participate is . . .*

- *Another way to participate is . . .*

CHECK IN  1  2  3  4

# The Birth of American Democracy

Literature Anthology:
pages 284–287

> 1     Every Fourth of July, Americans celebrate the birthday of the United States. Fireworks and parades remind us that the thirteen colonies declared independence from Great Britain on July 4, 1776. That birthday took place in Philadelphia, Pennsylvania. There, the Second Continental Congress approved the Declaration of Independence. This document formed a new nation, the United States of America. The Declaration is almost like our country's original birthday card.
>
> ## Our Founding Fathers
>
> 2     Five men, including John Adams, Thomas Jefferson, and Benjamin Franklin, wrote the Declaration of Independence. Jefferson wrote the first draft. His famous words sum up a basic American belief—"all men are created equal."

Reread paragraph 1. **Underline** two details that explain why the Fourth of July is called America's birthday.

COLLABORATE

Talk with a partner about how the author describes the Declaration of Independence. **Draw a circle** around the text evidence.

In paragraph 2, **put a checkmark** next to the line that tells what Thomas Jefferson believed. Write it here.

_____

_____

3  The men who signed the Declaration are called the Founding Fathers of our country. Signing the Declaration put the founders' lives in danger. They knew that their signatures made them traitors to Great Britain. They also knew that, if the colonies won the war, their names would go down in history.

4  Led by General George Washington, the colonists fought passionately for their freedom. After a long, bloody war, the British surrendered in 1781, and a peace treaty was signed in 1783. Our new nation was still a work in progress, however. Americans disagreed about how much power a federal, or central, government should have. Given that they had just won freedom from a powerful British king, Americans did not want their government to have too much power.

Reread paragraph 3. **Underline** the details that tell you how the Declaration of Independence was both risky and positive for the Founding Fathers. Write it here.

_____

_____

_____

COLLABORATE

Reread paragraph 4. Talk with a partner about how the author shows how the colonists felt about freedom. **Circle** the text evidence.

**Why is "The Birth of American Democracy" a good title for this selection?**

**Talk About It** Reread the excerpts on pages 142 and 143. Talk about why the Fourth of July is such an important holiday.

**Cite Text Evidence** What words and phrases show how our government was created? Write text evidence in the chart. Explain the author's purpose for presenting these details.

**Quick Tip**

Look for specific details or ideas in the text that tell you what happened on July 4, 1776. The details or ideas are important to the meaning of the author's purpose.

| Text Evidence | Author's Purpose |
|---|---|
|  |  |

**Write** "The Birth of American Democracy" is a good title because _____

_____

_____

_____

CHECK IN ⟩ 1 ⟩ 2 ⟩ 3 ⟩ 4 ⟩

# Homophones and Homographs

**Homophones** are two words that *sound* the same but are spelled differently and have different meanings.

- Examples: Pull the thread <u>through</u> the needle. He <u>threw</u> the ball.

**Homographs** are words that are *spelled* the same but have different meanings and origins. Use context clues to figure out the meanings of homographs.

- Examples: The <u>wind</u> blows. <u>Wind</u> the string around your finger.

 **FIND TEXT EVIDENCE**

On page 143 in paragraph 3, the author uses the homophone *their* and the homograph *lives*. The context of each sentence can help readers understand the word's meaning and how to pronounce it.

> Signing the Declaration put the founders' lives in danger. They knew that their signatures made them traitors to Great Britain.

 **Your Turn** Reread the first paragraph on page 142.

- Find a word that can be a homograph and write its two meanings. _____

  _____

- What word also has a homophone? Write the word and its

  homophone. _____

  _____

**Readers to Writers**

When you write, make sure to use the correct spelling of any words that are homophones. For example, these homophones are frequently confused: *their, there, they're*. Write a sentence for each homophone. Explain why you used that homophone.

**CHECK IN** 1 ⟩ 2 ⟩ 3 ⟩ 4 ⟩

**?** How do *See How They Run,* "The Birth of American Democracy," and the lyrics below from "Drill, Ye Tarriers" help you understand the need for government? How does government protect people's rights?

COLLABORATE

**Talk About It** Tarriers are people who waste time. In the song, the tarriers are the railroad workers who can't work quickly enough to meet the foreman's demands. Read the lyrics. Do you think what the foreman did is fair? Do you think there should be laws that protect workers and make sure they are treated fairly? Talk with a partner about how government can help to protect Jim Goff.

**Cite Text Evidence Circle** words and phrases that tell how the foreman treated Jim Goff.

**Write** *See How They Run,* "The Birth of American Democracy," and "Drill, Ye Tarriers" show how government is important because _____

_____

_____

_____

## from Drill, Ye Tarriers

Now, our new foreman was Jerry
   McCann,

You can bet that he was sure a
   blame mean man,

Last week a premature blast went off,

And a mile in the air went big Jim Goff,

Now, next time payday come around,

Jim Goff a dollar short was found,

When asked what for, came this reply,

"You were docked for the time you were
   up in the sky!"

CHECK IN  1  2  3  4

**My Goal** I know why we need government.

## Give a Speech

Think about what you learned about why we need government. How would you explain the need for government to other students?

**1** Look at your Build Knowledge notes in your reader's notebook.

**2** Make a list of reasons telling why we need government. Use information and examples from the texts you read.

**3** Use your list to write a speech telling why we need government. When you write, think about who your audience is. Start your speech with a hook to engage your audience. When you are done, practice giving your speech. Use new vocabulary words in your speech.

Think about what you learned in this text set. Fill in the bars on page 125.

# Build Knowledge

# Build Vocabulary

Write new words you learned about how inventions and technology affect our lives. Draw lines and circles for the words you write.

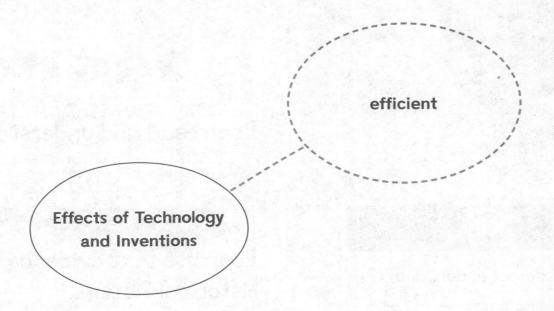

efficient

Effects of Technology and Inventions

Go online to **my.mheducation.com** and read the "Technology Today" Blast. Think about the technology you use. How does technology affect our everyday lives? Then blast back your response.

Think about what you already know. Fill in the bars. It's okay if you want more practice.

## What I Know Now

**Key**

| | |
|---|---|
| **1** = | I do not understand. |
| **2** = | I understand but need more practice. |
| **3** = | I understand. |
| **4** = | I understand and can teach someone. |

I can read and understand historical fiction.

1 > 2 > 3 > 4

I can use text evidence to respond to historical fiction.

1 > 2 > 3 > 4

I know how inventions and technology affect our lives.

1 > 2 > 3 > 4

**STOP** You will come back to the next page later.

Think about what you learned.
Fill in the bars. What progress did you make?

# What I Learned

I can read and understand historical fiction.

1  2  3  4

I can use text evidence to respond to historical fiction.

1  2  3  4

I know how inventions and technology affect our lives.

1  2  3  4

**My Goal** I can read and understand historical fiction.

## TAKE NOTES

As you read, make note of interesting words and important details.

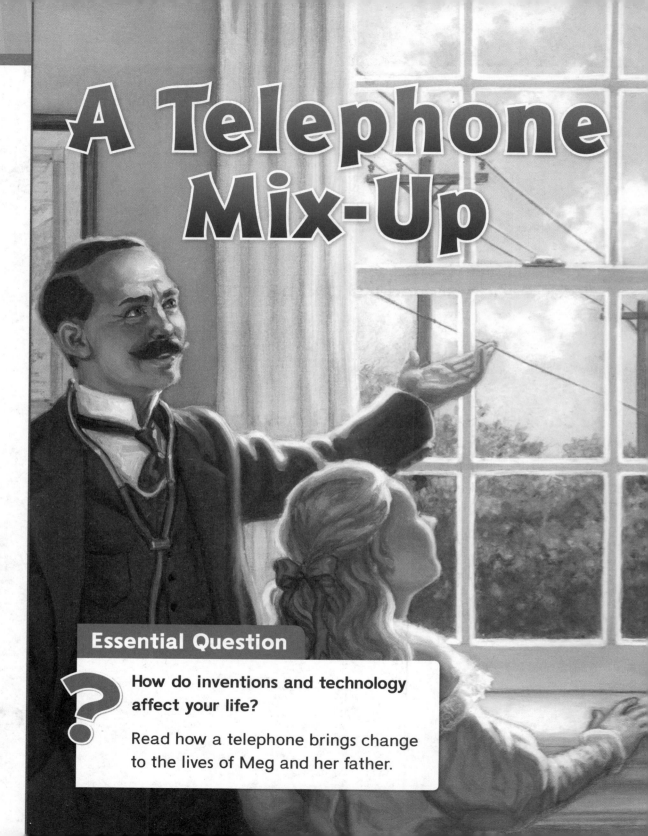

# A Telephone Mix-Up

### Essential Question

**?** How do inventions and technology affect your life?

Read how a telephone brings change to the lives of Meg and her father.

"By tomorrow afternoon there will be eight telephones right here in Centerburg, Ohio, and one of them will be ours!" Dr. Ericksen said to his daughter, Meg. "I predict that before this **decade** is over, in just another five years, there could be a hundred! That's how fast I foresee this **technology** will spread! When people need help, they'll call me on the telephone. Envision how many lives it will save! Picture all the amazing benefits!"

Meg realized that not everyone thought the telephone was an **engineering** marvel. She had heard people say that telephones were a useless invention. A few others felt the newfangled machine would open up a Pandora's box of troubles, causing people to stop visiting each other and writing letters.

Despite the concerns of some people, progress marched on. Just weeks earlier, Centerburg's first telephone had been installed in Mr. Kane's general store, another was put in at the hotel, and yet another at the newspaper office. Mrs. Kane was the town's first switchboard operator, **directing** incoming calls to the correct lines.

The next morning, Meg wrote "October 9, 1905" on the top of her slate with chalk while she **squirmed** in her seat, wishing that the long school day was over.

## FIND TEXT EVIDENCE

**Read**

Paragraphs 1–4
### Narrator's Point of View
**Circle** text that shows the story is being told from the third-person point of view.

Paragraphs 1–4
### Setting
**Draw a box** around the details that tell the setting of the story.

Paragraphs 2–4
### Make Predictions
**Underline** words that tell how people feel about the telephone. Predict how they will react when the town gets the telephones.

**Reread**
## Author's Craft

How does the word *squirmed* help you understand how Meg feels?

## FIND TEXT EVIDENCE

**Read**

▼

**Paragraphs 1–2**

### Character Perspective

**Draw a box** around how Meg thinks the telephone will affect her life.

### Synonyms

**Underline** the phrase that is a synonym for the word *scouted*. Write the phrase on the line.

_____

_____

**Paragraphs 3–8**

### Setting

**Circle** the text that tells you that the story takes place at a time when the telephone was a new invention that still had problems.

**Reread**

### Author's Craft

How does the author use dialogue to help you understand the relationship between Meg and her father?

Walking home that afternoon, Meg **scouted** the street, looking for the tall wooden poles that were going up weekly. Thick wire linked one pole to another, and Meg imagined how each wire would carry the words of friends and neighbors, their conversations zipping over the lines bringing news, birthday wishes, and party invitations.

As Meg hurried into the house, she let the screen door slam shut behind her. There on the wall was the **gleaming** wooden telephone box with its heavy black receiver on a hook. Her father was smiling broadly while **tinkering** with the shiny brass bells on top. "Isn't it a beauty?" he asked. "Have you ever seen such magnificence?"

Suddenly the telephone jangled loudly, causing both Ericksens to jump.

Meg laughed as her father picked up the receiver and shouted, "Yes, hello, this is the doctor!"

"Again please, Mrs. Kane! There's too much static!" Dr. Ericksen shouted. "I didn't get the first part. Bad cough? Turner farm?"

"Can I go, Father?" Meg asked as Dr. Ericksen returned the receiver to the hook.

"Absolutely," he said, grabbing his medical kit and heading outside where his horse and buggy waited.

When they got to the farm, they found Mr. Turner walking toward the barn.

"Jake, I got here as quick as I could," Dr. Ericksen said. "Is it Mrs. Turner? Little Emma?"

"You?" Jake Turner looked confused, but he gestured them toward the barn.

There they found a baby goat curled near its mother. The baby snorted, coughed, and looked miserable.

"Jake, I'm no vet!" said Dr. Ericksen. "You need Dr. Kerrigan."

"I was wondering why you showed up instead. I reckon there was a mix-up."

"Apparently so," Dr. Ericksen laughed. "When I get back, I'll send Dr. Kerrigan."

As years passed, the telephone proved to be very useful to the town of Centerburg, but there was always the occasional mix-up. It became common among the Ericksens to refer to a missed communication as "another sick goat."

## Summarize

Use your notes to Summarize the important events in "A Telephone Mix-Up."

## FIND TEXT EVIDENCE

Read

Paragraphs 1–4

**Character Perspective**

**Underline** the feeling that Mr. Turner has when he sees Dr. Ericksen.

Paragraphs 5–7

**Make Inferences**

**Circle** how the telephone affected Centerburg. What can you infer about the kinds of mix-ups the town experienced?

_____

_____

_____

_____

Reread

**Author's Craft**

How does the sick goat contribute to the plot?

# Vocabulary

**Use the example sentences to talk with a partner about each word. Then answer the questions.**

### decade
Rosa's family celebrated a **decade** of living in their home.

What will you be doing in a decade?

_____

_____

### directing
Two police officers were **directing** traffic.

If you were a crossing guard, what would you be directing students to do?

_____

_____

### engineering
I think the beautiful Golden Gate Bridge is an amazing example of **engineering**.

What is another amazing example of engineering?

_____

_____

### gleaming
The **gleaming** sun warmed the swimmers at the park.

What is an antonym for *gleaming*?

_____

_____

### scouted
They used binoculars as they **scouted** the best place to find birds.

What have you scouted in the park?

_____

_____

 **Build Your Word List** Choose an interesting word you noted on page 152 and look up the word's pronunciation and definition in a print or digital dictionary. Write the meaning in your reader's notebook and list one synonym for the word.

## squirmed

The kitten wiggled and **squirmed** in the girl's arms.

Why might the kitten have squirmed?

_____

_____

## technology

In the early 1900s, the telephone was considered new **technology**.

What are some examples of new technology in this century?

_____

_____

## tinkering

Mrs. Lan likes **tinkering** with broken bikes.

What is a synonym for *tinkering*?

_____

_____

## Synonyms

If a word is unfamiliar to you as you read, it might help to keep reading. Sometimes the author uses another word or phrase nearby that is close in meaning to the unfamiliar word. Words that have the same or similar meanings are **synonyms**.

### 🔍 FIND TEXT EVIDENCE

*As I read the first paragraph of "A Telephone Mix-Up" on page 153, I wasn't sure what the word* envision *meant. Then the word* picture *in the next sentence helped me figure out the meaning.*

Envision how many lives it will save! Picture all the amazing benefits!

**Your Turn** Use synonyms and other context clues to find the meanings of the following words in "A Telephone Mix-Up." Write a synonym and example sentence for each word.

**foresee**, page 153 _____

_____

**magnificence**, page 154 _____

_____

CHECK IN 〉 1 〉 2 〉 3 〉 4 〉

# Make Predictions

When you read, think about the genre and use text clues from the story to help you make predictions about what will happen next. As you continue to read, you can confirm or revise your predictions.

 **FIND TEXT EVIDENCE**

How did you predict the people of Centerburg would react to the telephone? What helped you to confirm your prediction? Reread page 153 of "A Telephone Mix-Up."

Page 153

Despite the concerns of some people, progress marched on. Just weeks earlier, Centerburg's first telephone had been installed in Mr. Kane's general store, another was put in at the hotel, and yet another at the newspaper office. Mrs. Kane was the town's first switchboard operator, directing incoming calls to the correct lines.

The next morning, Meg wrote "October 9, 1905" on the top of her slate with chalk while she squirmed in her seat, wishing that the long school day was over.

*I had predicted that people in Centerburg would get used to the telephone even though some people would not like the idea of it. Evidence in the paragraph confirmed my prediction.*

 **Your Turn** What text clues did you find that helped you predict that the phone would cause a mix-up? As you read, remember to use the strategy Make Predictions.

CHECK IN   1   2   3   4

# Plot: Setting

Historical fiction tells a story set in the past and is often based on real events. Historical fiction has realistic characters, events, dialogue, and settings. In historical fiction, the setting is usually very important to the plot, or what happens in the story.

## FIND TEXT EVIDENCE

*I can tell that "A Telephone Mix-Up" is historical fiction. A family is getting a telephone at a time in history when telephone service was first made available to many communities. The story has realistic characters, dialogue, events, and settings.*

Page 153

"By tomorrow afternoon there will be eight telephones right here in Centerburg, Ohio, and one of them will be ours!" Dr. Ericksen said to his daughter, Meg. "I predict that before this **decade** is over, in just another five years, there could be a hundred! That's how fast I foresee this **technology** will spread! When people need help, they'll call me on the telephone. Envision how many lives it will save! Picture all the amazing benefits!"

Meg realized that not everyone thought the telephone was an **engineering** marvel. She had heard people say that telephones were a useless invention. A few others felt the newfangled machine would open up a Pandora's box of troubles, causing people to stop visiting each other and writing letters.

Despite the concerns of some people, progress marched on. Just weeks earlier, Centerburg's first telephone had been installed in Mr. Kane's general store, another was put in at the hotel, and yet another at the newspaper office. Mrs. Kane was the town's first switchboard operator, **directing** incoming calls to the correct lines.

The next morning, Meg wrote "October 9, 1905" on the top of her slate with chalk while she **squirmed** in her seat, wishing that the long school day was over.

### Setting

Setting is the time and place of the story. The historical setting influences the plot and has an impact on characters.

**Your Turn** Choose an event in the story that is caused by the setting. Then tell how the event contributes to the plot._____

_____

_____

_____

_____

### Quick Tip

To better understand how setting contributes to the plot, think about what events are caused by the setting. Keep in mind that the setting affects the way the characters think and act, what they have, how they communicate, and how they travel.

CHECK IN  1  2  3  4

# Point of View and Perspective

The term *narrator's point of view* refers to the type of narrator telling the story. A first-person narrator is a character in the story. A third-person narrator is not in the story. We learn a character's *perspective*, or attitude toward something or someone, through what the narrator tells us about the character's thoughts, feelings, and actions.

 **FIND TEXT EVIDENCE**

*When I read page 153 of "A Telephone Mix-Up," I see that the narrator uses the pronoun she to tell what Meg is thinking. This tells me that the story has a third-person narrator. Paying attention to the details the narrator gives will help me understand Meg's perspective on the events in the story.*

| Details |
| --- |
| The narrator tells that Meg realizes that not everyone thinks the telephone is an "engineering marvel." |
| The narrator tells us that on the day the telephone is to arrive in Meg's home, Meg "squirmed in her seat, wishing the long school day was over." |

↓

| Character Perspective |
| --- |
| Despite what some other people think, Meg is excited about having a telephone. |

**Quick Tip**

A **first-person narrator** is in the story. Readers usually only know what the narrator knows. If the narrator uses pronouns such as *I, me, my,* and *our,* the narrator has a first-person point of view.

A **third-person narrator** is not in the story and can know the perspective of one or more characters.

 **Your Turn** Reread "A Telephone Mix-Up." Find details given by the narrator that show Dr. Ericksen's perspective about the telephone. Use the graphic organizer on page 161 to list the details.

CHECK IN 〉 1 〉 2 〉 3 〉 4 〉

| Details |
| --- |
| |
| |

↓

| Character Perspective |
| --- |
| |

**I can use text evidence to respond to historical fiction.**

# Respond to Reading

Discuss the prompt below. Use your notes and text evidence to support your response.

How does setting contribute to the story's plot?

_____

_____

_____

_____

_____

_____

_____

_____

_____

_____

_____

_____

## Quick Tip

Use these sentence starters to discuss the text and explain your answer.

- *In the story, the historical setting is . . .*
- *The main story event is . . .*
- *The historical setting affects the events in the story because . . .*

## Readers to Writers

When you write about a literary text, make sure to use the present tense to describe what happens even if the story is told in the past tense.

**Correct**: Dr. Ericksen *goes* to the Turner farm.

**Incorrect**: Dr. Ericksen *went* to the Turner farm.

**CHECK IN** 〉 1 〉 2 〉 3 〉 4 〉

# Technological Advances

COLLABORATE

Technological advances can affect many different aspects, or parts, of life. Create a three-column chart showing three different technological advances and their effect on your state. Work with a partner as you follow the research process and gather information to make the chart.

| Technological Advances in My State | | |
|---|---|---|
| Technological Advance | Date | Effect on My State |
| | | |
| | | |
| | | |

**Step 1** **Set a Goal** Choose three different technological advances that have had an effect on your state. Examples of technological advances include the steam engine, railroads, highway systems, bridges, and the delivery of water from one region to another. List questions you want your research to answer.

**Step 2** **Identify Sources** Use books and websites to find information about these technological advances and their effects on your state.

**Step 3** **Find and Record Information** Find information in your sources and take notes. Look for answers to the research questions you listed. Include information about when each technological advance first came about, as well as its effect on your state. Consider including images in your chart. Remember to cite your sources.

**Step 4** **Organize and Synthesize Information** Organize your notes and images. Create a rough draft of your chart.

**Step 5** **Create and Present** Revise your rough draft to create a final chart. After you finish, share your work with the class.

**Tech Tip**

You can find photographs and illustrations online for your chart. Be sure to use websites that are reliable. Usually, websites for reliable organizations end with *.gov*, *.edu*, or *.org*. Ask a librarian or other adult for suggestions. Remember to give credit to the websites where you found the images.

CHECK IN 1 2 3 4

# The Moon Over Star

 **How does the author help you understand how Gramps feels about the moon landing being shown on television?**

*Literature Anthology: pages 288–303*

**Talk About It** Reread **Literature Anthology** page 294. Turn to a partner and discuss Gramps's reaction to the moon landing on television.

**Cite Text Evidence** What words and phrases show how everyone reacts to Gran's announcement? Write text evidence and explain what it shows.

| Response to Gran's Announcement | What This Shows |
|---|---|
|  |  |
|  |  |
|  |  |
|  |  |

**Write** I know how Gramps feels about the moon landing because the author _____

_____

_____

 **Make Inferences**

You can learn about characters by their reactions to events or situations. Think about the historic setting, the moment in time in which the story takes place. What inferences can you make about Gramps from his reaction to the historic moon landing? What is important to him?

**Evaluate Information**

Rereading the text will help you understand how the setting affects a story. "The Moon Over Star" takes place at an important moment in history. How would the story be different if it did not have this historic setting?

**CHECK IN** ⟩ 1 ⟩ 2 ⟩ 3 ⟩ 4 ⟩

**?** How does the author use words and phrases to help you visualize the mood of that summer night?

**Talk About It** Reread **Literature Anthology** page 298. Talk with a partner about the author's description of the family's time outside at night. Discuss how that description makes you feel.

**Cite Text Evidence** What phrases help you picture what that night was like? Write text evidence in the chart.

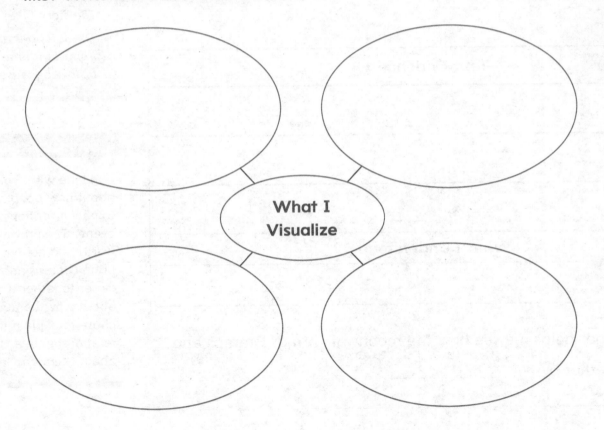

What I Visualize

CHECK IN  1  2  3  4

**How does the moonwalk bring Gramps and Mae closer together?**

**Talk About It** Reread the last paragraph on page 300 of the **Literature Anthology**. Turn to a partner and talk about how Gramps reacts to what the family is watching on television.

**Cite Text Evidence** What does Gramps say and do? Write text evidence and tell how his actions help you understand how he now feels about the moonwalk.

| Text Evidence |
| --- |
| |
| |
| |
| **What I Understand** |
| |

**Write** The author helps me see how the moonwalk brings Gramps and Mae closer together by _____

_____

_____

**Synthesize Information**

Combine what you know about how people respond to new inventions or events. Then review the words and actions that bring Gramps and Mae closer together. Think about why the author chose to explain their relationship in a story about the moon landing.

CHECK IN  1  2  3  4

# Respond to Reading

COLLABORATE

Discuss the prompt below. Use your notes and text evidence to support your ideas.

What can readers learn through Mae's experience with the moon landing?

_____
_____
_____
_____
_____
_____
_____
_____
_____
_____
_____
_____
_____
_____

## Quick Tip

Use these sentence starters to talk about the prompt and organize your ideas.

- *The story takes place . . .*
- *Readers learn that . . .*
- *Another example is . . .*
- *Mae learns that . . .*

Anson Ki/iStock/Getty Images

# Star Parties

Literature Anthology:
pages 306–309

### Find a Star Party

1. For decades, many national parks and observatories in the United States have held star parties. These are great locations for star parties because they can provide total darkness. . . .

2. Park rangers and astronomers will guide you through the night sky. They will point out and explain the different objects in the sky. There may be sights that are impossible to see where you live. . . .

3. Observatories have powerful technology that astronomers use to do their research. The McDonald Observatory in Texas is located in the Davis Mountains. At the observatory, star parties are held at a telescope park. The park has dome structures with different-sized telescopes. One dome has a 24-inch telescope that can be operated by a robot in a remote location—now that's great engineering!

Reread paragraph 1. **Underline** why national parks and observatories are great places for star parties.

Reread paragraph 2. **Draw a box** around the two things park rangers and astronomers do at star parties. Write them here.

_____

_____

_____

_____

**COLLABORATE**

Reread paragraph 3. Discuss the importance of the McDonald Observatory. **Circle** why it is "great engineering."

## What to See

1.  During different times of the year, you will get good views of some of the planets in our solar system. Many star gazers look for the largest planet, Jupiter, with its moons and rings. But if you want to see larger and brighter rings, look for Saturn in the night sky.

2.  There are also numerous constellations. A constellation is a group of stars that form a pattern or image. For example, Orion the Hunter is a constellation that the ancient Greeks thought looked like a hunter with a sword attached to its belt.

3.  At a star party you may get a chance to make a wish under a shooting star, or a meteor. Meteors are not really stars. They are bits of rocks. But they appear in the sky as beautiful streaks of light. When there are many shooting stars in the sky, it is called a meteor shower.

4.  No matter what time of year you go to a star party, you will not be disappointed. There is always something fascinating to see in the night sky.

Reread paragraph 1. **Circle** some of the things people can see in the night sky.

COLLABORATE

Look at the diagram and read the caption. Discuss when you can view the different phases of the Moon. How does the Sun affect the way we see the Moon?

_____

_____

_____

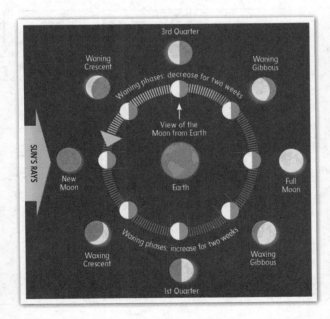

The Moon does not have a light source. When we see the Moon in the night sky, the Sun is shining on it. The Sun's light is reflecting off the Moon's surface.

**?** **What is the author's perspective on star parties?**

**Talk About It** Reread the excerpts on pages 168 and 169. Discuss what you can see and learn from star parties.

**Cite Text Evidence** What is the author's perspective on what you can see at star parties? Write text evidence in the chart.

| Detail | Detail | Detail |
|--------|--------|--------|
|        |        |        |

**Author's Perspective**

**Write** The author's perspective on star parties is _____

_____

_____

_____

CHECK IN  1  2  3  4

# Description

Authors can use a **description text structure** to help readers understand and visualize a topic or idea. A description text structure usually begins with the topic or idea, and then gives features, characteristics, or examples of the topic or idea.

 **FIND TEXT EVIDENCE**

On page 169, in paragraph 2, the topic is constellations. The author helps readers understand what a constellation is by telling a characteristic of constellations. Constellations "form a pattern or image." Then the author gives an example of a constellation to help readers visualize what is meant by "pattern or image."

> A constellation is a group of stars that form a pattern or image. For example, Orion the Hunter is a constellation that the ancient Greeks thought looked like a hunter with a sword attached to its belt.

**Your Turn** Read the inset "Phases of the Moon" on **Literature Anthology** page 308.

- What is topic? _____

- How does the author help you understand the topic? _____

_____

_____

A description text structure describes something. For example, it might describe what something looks like, what it does, where it is, or how it works.

Signal words and phrases including *for example*, *such as*, *feature*, and *characteristics* can help readers identify the descriptions.

How can you use a description text structure in your own writing?

**?** How do the photograph below and the selections *The Moon Over Star* and "Star Parties" help you understand the ways technology affects us?

**Talk About It** Look at the photograph and read the caption. Talk with a partner about what Claudia Mitchell is able to do with her prosthetic arm.

**Cite Text Evidence** Think about how technology has made Claudia's life better. **Circle** clues in the photograph that show what Claudia can do with her prosthetic arm. **Underline** evidence in the caption that shows how she controls her new arm.

**Write** The photograph and the selections help me understand the ways technology affects us by _____

_____

_____

_____

_____

_____

_____

In 2006, Claudia Mitchell was the first woman to receive a thought-controlled bionic arm. If she wants to pick something up, all she has to do is think about what she wants her prosthesis to do, and it does what she thinks.

> **Quick Tip**
>
> Use the photograph to tell about how technology can affect our lives. Use these sentence starters.
>
> • *The woman's bionic arm can . . .*
>
> • *She can use it to . . .*
>
> • *Bionic arms are a useful technology because . . .*

**CHECK IN** 1 2 3 4

**My Goal** I know how inventions and technology affect our lives.

## Write a Short Story

Think about what you learned about how inventions and technology affect people's lives. What effects did you find interesting or surprising?

**1** Look at your Build Knowledge notes in your reader's notebook.

**2** Using the information from the texts you read, make a list of ways inventions and technology affect people's lives.

**3** Use that list to write a quick short story about the effect of an invention or other technology. It could be about the effect on a place, on characters, or anything else that makes sense. Your story can take place in any time period. Use new vocabulary words in your story.

Think about what you learned in this text set. Fill in the bars on page 151.

# Build Knowledge

## Essential Question

**How do writers look at success in different ways?**

# Build Vocabulary

Write new words you learned about different ways of being successful. Draw lines and circles for the words you write.

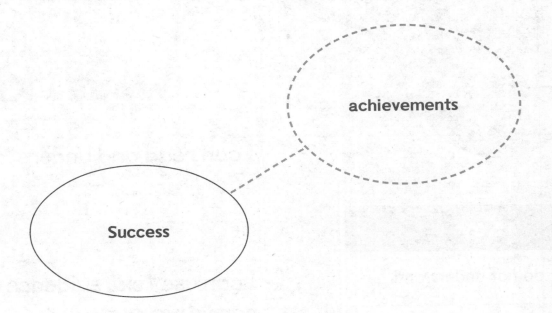

achievements

Success

Go online to **my.mheducation.com** and read the "Defining Success" Blast. Think about the things that inspire you. Where do you find inspiration to be successful? Then blast back your response.

Think about what you already know. Fill in the bars. Let's keep learning!

### Key

**1** = I do not understand.

**2** = I understand but need more practice.

**3** = I understand.

**4** = I understand and can teach someone.

# What I Know Now

I can read and understand narrative poetry.

| 1 | 2 | 3 | 4 |

I can use text evidence to respond to narrative poetry.

I know how writers look at success in different ways.

| 1 | 2 | 3 | 4 |

 You will come back to the next page later.

# What I Learned

I can read and understand narrative poetry.

I can use text evidence to respond to narrative poetry.

| 1 | 2 | 3 | 4 |

I know how writers look at success in different ways.

| 1 | 2 | 3 | 4 |

**My Goal** I can read and understand narrative poetry.

### TAKE NOTES

As you read, make note of interesting words and important details.

_____

_____

_____

_____

_____

_____

_____

_____

_____

_____

_____

_____

_____

### Sing to Me

### Essential Question

**How do writers look at success in different ways?**

Read about how two poets share stories of success.

The cool white keys stretched for miles.
How would my hands pull
and sort through the notes,
blending them into music?

I practiced
and practiced all day.
My fingers reaching for a melody
that hung dangling,
like an apple just out of reach.

*I can't do this.*
*I can't do this.*

The day ground on,
notes leaping hopefully into the air,
hovering briefly, only to crash,
an awkward jangle, a tangle of noise
before slowly fading away.

My mom found me, forehead on the keys.
She asked, "Would you like some help?
It took months for my hands to do what I wanted."
She sat down on the bench,
her slender fingers plucking notes
from the air.

*I can do this.*
*I can do this.*

She sat with me every night that week,
working my fingers until their efforts
made the keys sing to me, too.
                                        — Will Meyers

(bkgd) Tony Anderson/The Image Bank/Getty Images; (texture) Vincenzo Lombardo/Photographer's Choice RF/GettyImages; (tr) Mark Tomalty/Masterfile

## NARRATIVE POETRY

### FIND TEXT EVIDENCE

**Read**

Stanzas 1–4
**Character**

**Circle** the stanzas that tell how the speaker feels and sounds when playing the piano. What sentence summarizes his feelings?

_____

**Connotation and Denotation**

**Underline** a word in stanza 4 with a negative connotation, or feeling. Write what it means.

_____

_____

Stanzas 5–7
**Theme**

**Draw a box** around the stanza that helps to show the message of the poem.

**Reread**

### Author's Craft

With a partner, discuss the poet's use of the lines "*I can do this.*" and "*I can't do this.*"

## FIND TEXT EVIDENCE

**Read**

Stanzas 1–5

### Theme

**Circle** what the brother says to annoy the speaker.

**Draw a box** around what the speaker does as she waits for the bus. What does this tell you about the speaker?

_____

_____

### Connotation and Denotation

What does the use of the word *immense* in stanza 1 tell you about the speaker's feelings about the tree?

_____

_____

_____

What is the literal, or actual, meaning of *immense*?

_____

_____

**Reread**

### Author's Craft

How does the poet use repetition to support the theme of the poem?

# The Climb

"Go on, I dare you!" My brother's voice
mocking, a jaybird's repetitive screech.
We are waiting for the bus
under our immense oak tree.

I reach for the lowest branch and find
another to pull myself up before
I lose my grip on the slippery bark
and slither down the trunk. Again.

Today, at school,
I drop my milk at lunch,
take a pop quiz,
and argue with my friends.

Today is my birthday.
When I get off the bus,
The oak tree doesn't look
any smaller or bigger.

Today, I am ten years old.
I reach for the lowest branch
and find another to pull myself up.
My hands find another and another.

Over and over among the red
outstretched leaves,
foot to branch: push!
hand to branch: pull!

My brother is rooted on the ground,
staring up at me,
until finally, I can't climb any higher,
or I will be a cloud.

— Sonya Mera

## Make Connections

Compare how the characters in each poem feel to how you feel when you are successful.

**Stanzas 6–7**
### Structure

**Circle** the words the poet repeats in stanza 6. What effect does the repetition have?

_____

_____

### Theme

**Underline** the action words in stanza 6 that help tell the poem's theme, or message.
Write the words on the lines.

_____

Reread
## Author's Craft

What image does the poet use to describe the speaker's brother?

# Vocabulary

**Use the example sentences to talk with a partner about each word. Then answer the questions.**

### attain

The mountain climber wanted to **attain** the goal of being the first person to reach the peak.

What goal would you like to attain?

_____

_____

### dangling

The ripe apple was **dangling** from the end of the branch.

What are some things you might find dangling?

_____

_____

### hovering

The hummingbird was **hovering** in front of the flower's petals.

Write a sentence about something you have seen hovering.

_____

_____

### triumph

Winning the state championship was a **triumph**!

What is a synonym for _triumph_?

_____

# Poetry Terms

### stanza

A **stanza** is one or more lines in a poem that form a unit of the poem.

Explain how you know when a stanza ends.

_____

_____

### repetition

Poets who repeat words or phrases in a poem are using **repetition**.

How might repetition add to a poem's meaning?

_____

_____

### denotation

The **denotation** is the basic definition of a word. It is an example of literal language.

What is the denotation of the word *little?*

_____

_____

### connotation

The **connotation** is a meaning suggested by a word in addition to its literal meaning.

What is the connotation of the words *scrawny cat?*

_____

_____

> **Build Your Word List** Reread "Sing to Me" on page 179. Underline three words that look interesting to you. In your reader's notebook, write the three words. Use an online or print thesaurus to find two synonyms for each word. Write a sentence using one of the synonyms for each word.

## Connotation and Denotation

**Connotation** is a feeling or idea connected to a word.

**Denotation** is the dictionary's definition of a word.

### 🔍 FIND TEXT EVIDENCE

*When I read "Sing to Me" on page 179, I know that some words suggest positive or negative feelings. The denotation of the word* slender *is "thin."* Slender *has a positive connotation, as in "long and elegant."* Slender *is very different from the word* scrawny, *even though the denotation for both is "thin."*

**She sat down on the bench, her slender fingers plucking notes from the air.**

**Your Turn** Reread "The Climb" on pages 180-181. What are the definition and feeling of the word *screech*? In your reader's notebook, write the word, its denotation, and its connotation.

You can look for context clues—other words around it—to help you figure out the connotation of a word.

_____

_____

CHECK IN ▶ 1 ▶ 2 ▶ 3 ▶ 4

Mark Tomalty/Masterfile

# Structure

A poem's **structure**, or organization, helps to create meaning in the poem. **Stanzas** are a part of a poem's structure. A stanza is one or more lines in a poem that form a unit in the poem. Each stanza expresses an idea. Together, these ideas contribute to the poem's theme, or message. A poem's structure might also include **repetition**, the repeating of words and phrases. Poets use repetition to emphasize images and ideas.

 **FIND TEXT EVIDENCE**

Reread the poem "The Climb" on pages 180-181. Identify the stanzas and listen for words and phrases that are repeated.

### Quick Tip

When poets repeat words, they want you to notice specific words or ideas. When you see a repeated word or phrase, ask yourself: "What is the important idea that the poet is telling me here?"

- The words repeated in "The Climb" are . . .

- The word Today begins three stanzas because . . .

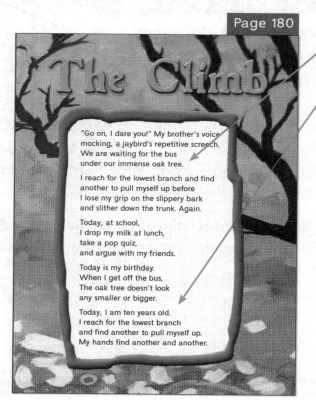

Page 180

The Climb

"Go on, I dare you!" My brother's voice
mocking, a jaybird's repetitive screech.
We are waiting for the bus
under our immense oak tree.

I reach for the lowest branch and find
another to pull myself up before
I lose my grip on the slippery bark
and slither down the trunk. Again.

Today, at school,
I drop my milk at lunch,
take a pop quiz,
and argue with my friends.

Today is my birthday.
When I get off the bus,
The oak tree doesn't look
any smaller or bigger.

Today, I am ten years old.
I reach for the lowest branch
and find another to pull myself up.
My hands find another and another.

**Stanza** Each of these groups of lines is a stanza.

**Repetition** The poet starts the last three stanzas on this page with "Today."

 **Your Turn** Reread "Sing to Me" on page 179. What two lines does the poet repeat in this poem? What effect does the repetition have?

COLLABORATE

_____

_____

_____

_____

_____

_____

CHECK IN 1 2 3 4

# Narrative Poetry

**Narrative poetry** tells a story and has characters. A narrative poem

- can be about fictional or real events
- may be written in stanzas
- may or may not have a rhyme scheme, or pattern of end rhymes.

 **FIND TEXT EVIDENCE**

I can tell that "Sing to Me" and "The Climb" are narrative poems because they both tell a story and have characters.

Page 179

> I practiced
> and practiced all day.
> My fingers reaching for a melody
> that hung dangling,
> like an apple just out of reach.

**Character**
The speaker of this poem is also a character in the poem. We see the events from his perspective.

**COLLABORATE**

**Your Turn** Reread the poem "The Climb" on pages 180–181. Identify the elements that tell you it is a narrative poem.

_____

_____

_____

_____

**Readers to Writers**

When you write a narrative poem, decide what narrative point of view you want to use. If you aren't sure, you can try first writing the poem from the first-person point of view—the speaker is a character in the poem. Use pronouns such as *I*, *me*, and *my*.

Then try rewriting the poem from the third-person point of view—the speaker is not a character in the poem. Use pronouns such as *he* or *she*.

How do the different narrative points of view affect the poem and what the readers learn about a character's perspective, or attitude, about someone or something?

**CHECK IN** 1 2 3 4

# Theme

Theme is the overall idea or message about life in a text. Sometimes a text can have more than one theme. To identify a theme in a poem and how it develops, pay attention to how the speaker reflects on, or thinks about, the poem's topic.

## 🔍 FIND TEXT EVIDENCE

*I'll reread "The Climb" on pages 180–181. I will look at the speaker's words and actions to help me identify the theme.*

| Detail |
|---|
| I lose my grip on the slippery bark / and slither down the trunk. Again. |

↓

| Detail |
|---|
| The oak tree doesn't look / any smaller or bigger. |

↓

| Detail |
|---|
| My hands find another and another. |

↓

| Theme |
|---|
| Persistence leads to success. |

**Your Turn** Reread "Sing to Me" on page 179. Find the important details and list them in the graphic organizer on page 187. Use the details to determine the theme of the poem. Explain your ideas to your partner.

COLLABORATE

**Quick Tip**

Usually, the theme of a poem is implied, or not directly stated. To find a theme, you can ask yourself:

- *What is the topic of the poem?*
- *How are things described? What are the connotations and denotations of the words used?*
- *What information or idea is in each stanza?*
- *If the poem is a narrative, what lesson do the speaker or characters in the poem learn?*

CHECK IN   1 > 2 > 3 > 4

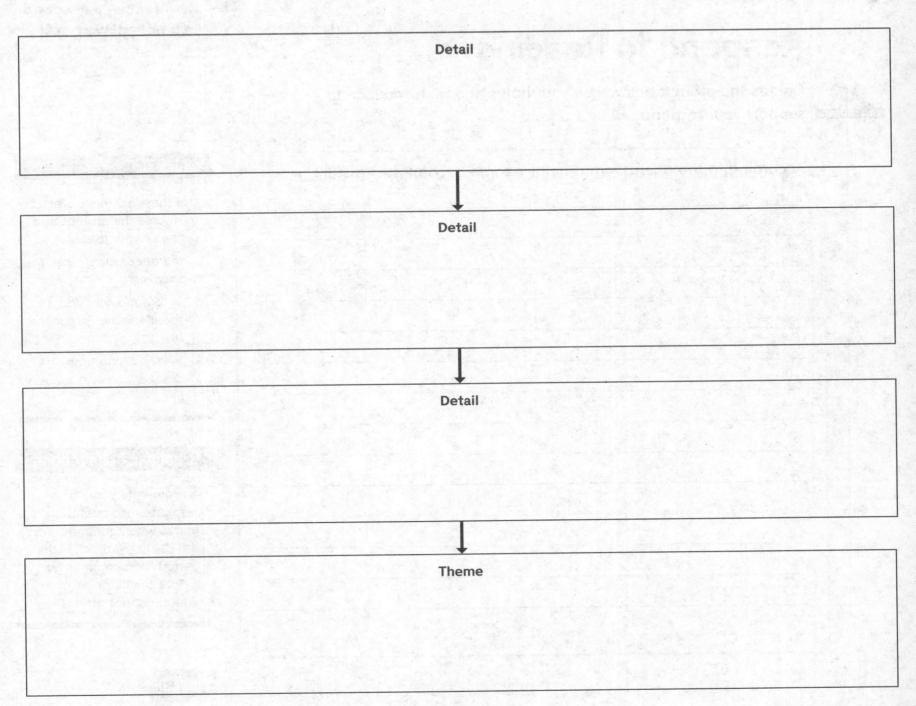

**Detail**

**Detail**

**Detail**

**Theme**

# Respond to Reading

Discuss the prompt below. Use your notes and text evidence to support your response.

According to the poems, what helps people become successful?

_____

_____

_____

_____

_____

_____

_____

_____

_____

_____

_____

_____

_____

## Quick Tip

Use these sentence starters to discuss the prompt and organize your ideas.

- *In both of the poems, the speakers . . .*
- *In "Sing to Me," the speaker achieves success by . . .*
- *In "The Climb," the speaker achieves success by . . .*

## Grammar Connections

As you write your response, use quotation marks when quoting from the poem. Remember that periods and commas go before the closing quotation, not after it.

CHECK IN 1 2 3 4

# Looking at Success

COLLABORATE

People look at success in different ways. How do you define success? Interview someone at school or at home that you consider successful. Find out how they achieved this success. Follow the research process as you plan and conduct your interview. Work with a partner.

This student is interviewing an adult who she thinks is successful. What questions do you think she might ask?

_____

_____

_____

**Step 1** **Set a Goal** Create a list of people at your school or at home that you think are successful. Remember that a person can be successful in any number of ways. Why do you think they are successful?

**Step 2** **Identify Sources** Narrow your list of people down to one person to interview. Think of questions to ask the person.

**Step 3** **Find and Record Information**
- Prepare your questions ahead of the interview.
- Practice asking the questions with a partner. Clarify any unclear questions.
- During the interview, take notes and listen closely. It's okay if you need to ask your interviewee to clarify answers.

 **Tech Tip**

If your interviewee agrees, use a laptop, tablet, or cell phone as a recording device. Be sure to place the device where both you and the interviewee can be heard clearly.

**Step 4** **Organize and Synthesize Information** Listen to the recording of the interview or reread notes you took. Look for any parts that are unclear or not focused on the topic and try to edit them out.

**Step 5** **Create and Present** Write an introduction that tells who your interviewee is and why you chose that person to interview. Decide how to present your interview.

Fuse/Getty Images

CHECK IN  1  2  3  4

# Swimming to the Rock

**?** **How does the poet help you visualize how the speaker feels as she watches her father and brothers swim?**

*Literature Anthology: pages 310–312*

COLLABORATE

**Talk About It** Reread stanzas 3–5 on pages 310 and 311 of the **Literature Anthology**. Talk with a partner about what the speaker's father and brothers are doing.

**Cite Text Evidence** What words and phrases show what the speaker sees as she watches them swim? Write text evidence in the chart.

 **Evaluate Information**

Sensory words relate to the things we can see, hear, touch, smell, and taste. Which sense does the poet use the most words to describe? How would the poem be different if the author did not use sensory words?

| Text Evidence | Why It's Important |
|---|---|
|  |  |
|  |  |
|  |  |

**Write** The poet helps me visualize how the narrator feels by _____

_____

_____

CHECK IN  1  2  3  4

# The Moondust Footprint

**?** **What words and phrases does the poet use to express the mood and feeling of the speaker?**

**Talk About It** Reread page 312 of the **Literature Anthology**. Talk with a partner about how the speaker describes the Moon landing.

**Cite Text Evidence** What words and phrases create mood? Write text evidence in the chart.

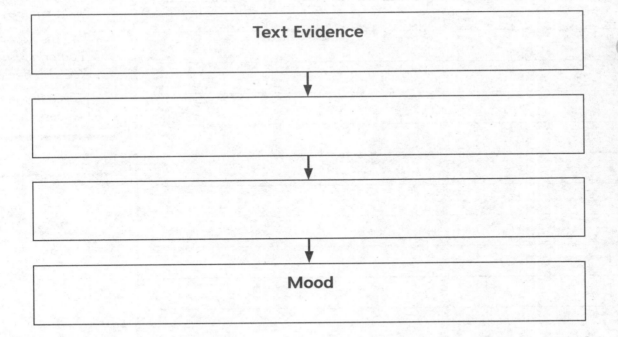

**Text Evidence**

**Mood**

**Write** The poet expresses the mood and feeling of the speaker by _____

_____

_____

**Quick Tip**

For a better understanding of how sensory words create a mood, use the sentence starters below.

- *During a rainstorm, I see . . .*
- *The rain sounds like . . .*
- *The rain smells like . . .*
- *The rain feels . . .*

**Synthesize Information**

Combine what you know about repetition and sensory words and images. Think of words or phrases to express how you felt about watching an exciting event. Use sensory words to describe your mood and the event.

**CHECK IN** 1 2 3 4

# Respond to Reading

Discuss the prompt below. Use your notes and text evidence to support your response.

COLLABORATE

What can readers learn about success from "Swimming to the Rock" and "The Moondust Footprint"?

_____

_____

_____

_____

_____

_____

_____

_____

_____

_____

_____

_____

**Quick Tip**

Use these sentence starters to talk about and cite text evidence.

- In "Swimming to the Rock," the speaker . . .

- In "The Moondust Footprint," the speaker feels . . . because . . .

- This tells me that success can be . . .

Apollo 11 Commander Neil A. Armstrong/NASA

CHECK IN  1  2  3  4

# Genius

**?** How does the poet use figurative language to help you understand what the speaker is like?

Literature Anthology:
pages 314–315

**Talk About It** Reread the last two stanzas on **Literature Anthology** page 314. Talk with a partner about what the speaker and his sister are doing.

**Cite Text Evidence** What words and phrases describe the speaker's sister? Write text evidence in the chart.

| Figurative Language | What I Understand |
|---|---|
|  |  |

**Write** The poet uses figurative language to help me understand _____

_____

_____

## Quick Tip

Figurative language includes idioms, hyperbole, similes, metaphors, and personification.

Figurative language can be used to compare two different things. Use these sentence starters to help you understand figurative language.

- *The narrator compares his sister to a . . .*

- *They are being compared because both are . . .*

# Winner

**?** **How does the poet help you understand how the speaker feels about his father?**

**Talk About It** Reread the last stanza on page 315 of the **Literature Anthology**. Talk with a partner about what the speaker says his dad does when he hits the ball.

**Cite Text Evidence** What phrases show how the speaker feels about his father? Write text evidence in the chart and tell how it helps you understand.

| Text Evidence | How It Helps |
|---|---|
|  |  |
|  |  |
|  |  |

**Write** I know how the speaker feels about his father because the poet

_____

_____

**CHECK IN** 1 2 3 4

# Rhyme and Structure

A poem's structure includes the arrangement of rhyming words and other sound patterns, as well as repetition, imagery, line breaks, and stanzas. Poets use rhyme and structure to create meaning by emphasizing certain actions, images, ideas, and feelings in their poems.

 **FIND TEXT EVIDENCE**

In "Genius" on page 314 in the **Literature Anthology**, the stanzas each have two lines. Each stanza focuses on an action or emotion involved with the speaker getting his sister's opinion of his poem. This focus emphasizes the importance of her opinion.

The last word of every two stanzas rhymes, which emphasizes certain ideas in the poem. For example, in the first two stanzas, the rhyming words *night* and *light* emphasize that the poem is taking place at night. The fact that the speaker wakes his sister late at night shows how important her opinion is to him.

 **Your Turn** Reread "Winner" on Literature Anthology page 315.

- What words rhyme in the first stanza? How does that create meaning in the poem?

_____

_____

- Why do you think there are two stanzas in the poem?

_____

_____

**?** Think about the poems you read this week. How does Douglas Malloch's description of success in the poem on this page compare to the ways the other poets describe, or look at, success?

COLLABORATE

**Talk About It** Read the poem. Talk with a partner about how the poem describes what it means to be a success.

**Cite Text Evidence** **Underline** words and phrases that show how the poet describes what success means. Put **checkmarks** in the margin beside text evidence where the poet is comparing two things.

**Write** Douglas Malloch and the poets I read this week describe success by _____

_____

_____

_____

_____

_____

_____

©nobeastsofierce Labels/Cockades collection/Alamy Stock Photo

from
## Be the Best of Whatever You Are

We can't all be captains, we've got to be crew,
    There's something for all of us here.
There's big work to do and there's lesser to do,
    And the task we must do is the near.
If you can't be a highway then just be a trail,
    If you can't be the sun be a star;
It isn't by size that you win or you fail—
    Be the best of whatever you are!

—by Douglas Malloch

CHECK IN ▶ 1 ⟩ 2 ⟩ 3 ⟩ 4

# SHOW YOUR KNOWLEDGE

My Goal: I know how writers look at success in different ways.

## Write a Poem

What did you learn about how writers look at success in different ways? How does this compare to your own ideas of success?

**1** Look at your Build Knowledge notes in your reader's notebook.

**2** Brainstorm a list of how the texts you read portray, or show, success. Cross off any ideas you don't agree with. Then add a few ideas of your own.

**3** Use your list to write a poem about what the word "success" means to you. Try to include new vocabulary. When you are done, create an illustration to go with your poem.

Think about what you learned in this text set. Fill in the bars on page 177.

# MY GOALS

Think about what you already know. Fill in the bars. It's important to keep learning.

## What I Know Now

I can write an expository essay.

| 1 | 2 | 3 | 4 |

I can synthesize information from four sources.

| 1 | 2 | 3 | 4 |

### Key

**1** = I do not understand.

**2** = I understand but need more practice.

**3** = I understand.

**4** = I understand and can teach someone.

Think about what you learned. Fill in the bars. What helped you do your best?

# What I Learned

I can write an expository essay.

1 > 2 > 3 > 4

I can synthesize information from four sources.

1 > 2 > 3 > 4

## WRITE TO SOURCES

You will answer an expository writing prompt using sources and a rubric.

## ANALYZE THE RUBRIC

A rubric tells you what needs to be included in your writing.

**Purpose, Focus, and Organization**

Read the fourth bullet. Why is it important to use a logical text structure to organize ideas?

_____

_____

_____

**Evidence and Elaboration**

Read the third bullet. How does using elaborative techniques such as examples and definitions support a central idea?

_____

_____

_____

_____

_____

_____

# Expository Writing Rubric

### Purpose, Focus, and Organization • Score 4

- stays focused on the purpose, audience, and task
- clearly presents and fully develops the central idea about a topic
- uses transitional strategies, such as words and phrases, to connect ideas
- **uses a logical text structure to organize information**
- begins with a strong introduction and ends with a strong conclusion

### Evidence and Elaboration • Score 4

- effectively supports the central idea with convincing facts and details
- has strong examples of relevant evidence, or supporting details, from multiple sources
- uses elaborative techniques, such as facts, examples, definitions, and quotations from sources
- expresses interesting ideas clearly using precise language
- uses appropriate academic and domain-specific language
- uses different sentence structures

Turn to page 240 for the complete Expository Writing Rubric.

# Logical Text Structure

**Organize Information** Good writers organize and present information in a way that is logical, or makes sense. They choose a text structure that will best help readers understand the information and how the ideas in different sentences and paragraphs are connected.

Compare and contrast is one kind of logical text structure. The information is organized to show how two or more things are alike or different. Transition words and phrases help readers to connect similarities and differences. These words and phrases include *alike, both, same, unlike, different, or, however, on the other hand,* and *but*.

> Cats and dogs make good pets. Dogs need to be let outside a few times a day. Cats can use a litter box. Dogs love to go for walks, play, and run around. Cats like to sleep for most of the day. They are quiet. Dogs can be loud because they bark.

Rewrite the paragraph above by combining sentences and adding words that signal a comparison or a contrast is being made. The first sentence is done for you.

Both cats and dogs make good pets. _____

_____

_____

_____

_____

# WRITING

## ANALYZE THE STUDENT MODEL

**Paragraphs 1–2**

**Draw a box** around the central idea in paragraph 1.

Read the two highlighted sentences. **Circle** the text that shows the connection between the first and second paragraphs. Now look at the rubric. What is the text an example of?

**Paragraph 3**

**Circle** three examples of domain-specific vocabulary in paragraph 3.

_____

_____

_____

**Underline** an example of elaboration in paragraph 3. Why is it important for younger people to vote?

_____

_____

_____

Mia responded to the Writing Prompt: *Write an expository essay for a school bulletin board display about why people vote.* Read Mia's essay below.

**1**   Do you ever wonder what the big deal is about voting in government elections? The answer is not mysterious. In America, voters choose many of the people in government. These elected officials make decisions such as how money is spent and what laws are passed. People vote to have a say about who is in the government and the decisions that are made.

**2**   In America, we vote to elect people who will represent us in government. However, elections are not just about voting for the president and members of Congress. We also vote in state elections. Residents of each state vote for their governor, state senators, and state representatives. They also vote for local government officials, such as county commissioners, city council members, and mayors.

**3**   Despite the fact that voting gives people a say in the government, some people don't believe their votes make a difference. According to "Young People Should Vote," people aged 18 to 29 are the least likely to vote. As one college student said, "It's not like my vote is going to matter." This is wrong. The more younger people vote, the more politicians will have to pay attention to them and what they want.

**4**     This ability to vote and choose government members is so important that people are willing to stand up and protest for this right. For example, when Victoria Woodhull ran for president of the United States in 1872, she could not vote for herself. Women did not have the right to vote. According to the article "Women in the White House," when Susan B. Anthony voted in that election, she was arrested. She was fined $100 for breaking the law! Women finally got the vote in 1920. Other Americans also had to struggle for the right to vote. Although African Americans could vote in 1870, many states would not let them. Native Americans were not allowed to vote until 1924, but even then, they couldn't vote in some states. The Voting Rights Act of 1965 finally protected the rights of all citizens to vote.

**5**     I can't vote yet, but I know that it is important to participate in voting for representatives that will make good decisions. In *See How They Run*, I read about the organization Kids Voting USA. It gets students involved in elections. And even though they are too young to vote, they can make sure their parents vote. I think that's a great idea. I can't wait until I'm old enough to vote!

**Paragraph 4**

**Underline** an example of elaboration in paragraph 4. What is the purpose of paragraph 4?

_____

_____

_____

**Paragraph 5**

**Underline** the sentence in the conclusion that restates Mia's central idea from paragraph 1.

**Apply the Rubric**

With a partner, use the rubric on page 200 to discuss why Mia scored a 4 on her essay.

Darrin Henry/Shutterstock

# Analyze the Prompt

## Writing Prompt

*Write an expository essay for your class comparing the three branches of the federal government to the three branches of state governments.*

**Purpose, Audience, and Task** Reread the writing prompt. What is your purpose for writing? My purpose is to _____

_____

Who will your audience be? My audience will be _____

_____

What type of writing is the prompt asking for? _____

_____

**Set a Purpose for Reading Sources** Asking questions about how the federal government and state governments are alike and different will help you figure out your purpose for reading. You will read a passage set about federal and state governments and the selection "The Birth of American Democracy" on pages 284–287 in the **Literature Anthology**. Before you begin reading, write a question below.

_____

_____

## EXPOSITORY ESSAY

*State Government:*
# The Executive Branch

1      State constitutions protect the rights of citizens and explain what the government does. Similar to the US Constitution, state constitutions divide the government into three separate branches: executive, legislative, and judicial. Each branch has some power over the other two branches. This system is called "checks and balances." The system makes sure that no one person or group gains too much power. **Let's take a look at what the executive branch does.**

2      **The governor is elected to head the executive branch.** He or she is responsible for carrying out state laws. Probably the most important job of the governor is to manage the state budget. He or she must create a plan for how the state will spend its money. For example, roads may need to be built or repaired. Then the governor needs to present the plan to the legislature.

3      The lieutenant governor and the cabinet are part of the executive branch in most states. The lieutenant governor helps with some of the governor's responsibilities. The people in the cabinet help the governor run the state government. Some of the people in the cabinet might include an attorney general, secretary of state, treasurer, commissioner of education, commissioner of agriculture, and comptroller. It takes many people with different skills to govern a state.

**FIND TEXT EVIDENCE** 🔍

**Paragraphs 1–2**
**Underline** a word in paragraph 1 that signals a comparison. How are the US Constitution and a state constitution alike?

_____

_____

Read the highlighted sentences. **Circle** two words in the second paragraph that help connect it to the first paragraph.

What is one of the most important jobs the governor does?

_____

_____

**Paragraph 3**
**Draw a box** around the details that tell you what the cabinet does. What might *govern* mean?

_____

📝 **Take Notes** Paraphrase the central idea of the source and give examples of details that support this idea.

**Paragraphs 4–5**

**Circle** the names of the two parts of the legislative branch. Read the highlighted sentences in paragraphs 4 and 5. What word or words appear in both sentences to help connect the paragraphs?

_____

_____

_____

**Underline** the details that tell you how a bill can still become law if the governor vetoes it.

**Paragraph 6**

If you have an idea for a state law, who can help you to turn it into a bill?

_____

_____

_____

**Take Notes** Paraphrase the central idea of the source and give examples of details that support this idea.

**SOURCE 2**

# State Government:
## The Legislative Branch

4    The legislative branch makes the laws for a state. In every state but Nebraska, the legislative branch has two parts: the Senate and the House of Representatives. The legislative branch is made up of elected representatives. Members of the Senate are called senators. Members of the House of Representatives are called state representatives. **These are the people who propose bills and vote on them.**

5    **For a bill to become a law, the majority of senators and representatives must vote to pass the bill.** A governor then either signs the bill into law or vetoes it. If the governor vetoes the bill, the bill can still become law. Legislators can try to override the veto. States have different rules about how to do this. In most states, a two-thirds vote from the House and the Senate is required to overturn the veto. If the legislature does not try to override the veto or does not succeed, then the bill dies. This means that the bill does not become a law.

6    Many people have ideas that they want to make into laws. But how does that happen? If a citizen, group, or legislator has an idea for a new law, a representative can turn it into a bill. So, if you have an idea for a law, present your idea to your state representative. She or he will decide if your idea should be a bill. By working with their representatives, all citizens can take part in the legislative process.

## State Government:
# The Judicial Branch

SOURCE 3

7    The judicial branch is the court system. It is made up of the supreme court, the district courts of appeals, the circuit courts, and the county courts. The judges and justices in the judicial branch make decisions about cases that are brought to the court. They review the cases' facts and interpret the law.

8    A state's supreme court is the highest court in the state. The number of justices on a state supreme court varies by state. There are between five and nine. The supreme court decides if laws passed by the legislative branch follow the rules of the state constitution. State supreme courts do not hear trials. They hear appeals, or cases that need to be reviewed.

### State Courts

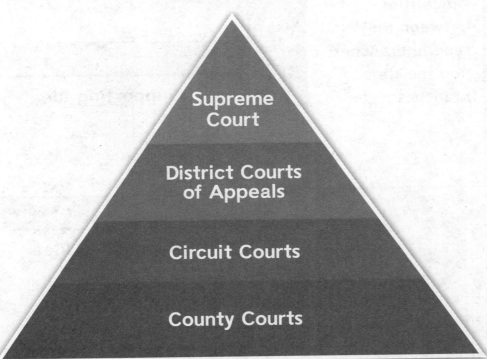

Supreme Court

District Courts of Appeals

Circuit Courts

County Courts

## FIND TEXT EVIDENCE

**Paragraph 7**

**Circle** the details that tell you the names of the different parts of the judicial branch in state governments.

**Underline** the details that tell about the role of the judicial branch.

**Paragraph 8**

How many justices serve on a state supreme court?

_____

_____

**Diagram**

What information does the chart provide?

_____

_____

_____

**Take Notes** Paraphrase the central idea of the source and give examples of details that support this idea.

# WRITING

**My Goal** I can synthesize information from four sources.

## TAKE NOTES

Read the writing prompt below. Then use the four sources, your notes, and the graphic organizer to plan a response.

**Writing Prompt** *Write an expository essay for your class comparing the three branches of the federal government to the three branches of state governments.*

### Synthesize Information

Review your notes for all four sources. What are the biggest differences between the federal government and state governments? Discuss your ideas with a partner.

CHECK IN ▶ 1 ⟩ 2 ⟩ 3 ⟩ 4

## Plan: Organize Ideas

**Introduction**

Both the federal government and state governments have three branches. There are many similarities between the federal branches and the state branches.

**Body**

**Supporting Idea**

State governments and the federal government both have an executive branch.

**Supporting Idea**

**Supporting Idea**

**Supporting Idea**

**Relevant Evidence**

The governor...

**Relevant Evidence**

**Relevant Evidence**

**Relevant Evidence**

**Conclusion**

# Draft: Elaboration

**Build on It** Writers use elaboration, such as facts, examples, quotations, and definitions, to support the central idea in a text. These elaborative techniques also help readers to better understand the topic. Read the paragraph about petitions. Look for an example of elaboration.

### Grammar Connections

As you write your draft, be aware of homophones. For example, you might write *state capital* instead of *state capitol*. Other frequently confused words are *to, too, two* and *their, there, they're*. Remember, a spell checker will not catch these kinds of errors.

> If there is a change you want to make in your community, you can create a petition. A petition is a document asking for a change. The word *petition* comes from the Latin root *petere*, which means "seek or request." Take your petition around to everyone you know and ask them to sign it. Then send the petition to your local or state government to show them that a lot of people feel the same way you do.

Underline the sentences that use elaboration. Then, look at the information in your graphic organizer on page 209. What is one elaborative technique that you are planning to use in your expository essay? Write your answer below.

_____

_____

_____

_____

**Draft** Use your graphic organizer to write your draft in your writer's notebook. Before you start writing, review the rubric on page 200. Remember to indent each paragraph.

**CHECK IN** 1 > 2 > 3 > 4

TrotzOlga/Shutterstock

# Revise: Peer Conferences

**Review a Draft** Listen actively to your partner. Take notes about what you liked and what was difficult to follow. Begin by telling what you liked. Use these sentence starters:

*I like the way you elaborated on this idea because . . .*
*What did you mean by . . .*
*I think adding an example . . .*

After you give each other feedback, reflect on the peer conference. What suggestion did you find the most helpful?

_____

_____

**Revision** Use the Revising Checklist to help you figure out what text you may need to move, elaborate on, or delete. After you finish writing your final draft, use the full rubric on pages 240–243 to score your essay.

## ✔ Revising Checklist

- ☐ Does my essay have a strong central idea?
- ☐ Did I present the information in a logical order?
- ☐ Did I include different types of elaborative techniques? Did I use facts, definitions, examples, or quotations?
- ☐ Did I check my grammar?
- ☐ Did I check my spelling and punctuation?

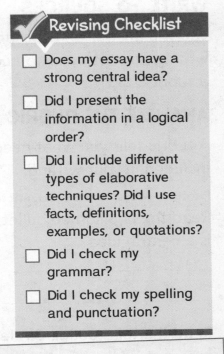

Next, you'll write an expository essay on a new topic.

## My Score

| Purpose, Focus, & Organization (4 pts) | Evidence & Elaboration (4 pts) | Conventions (2 pts) | Total (10 pts) |
|---|---|---|---|
|  |  |  |  |

## WRITE TO SOURCES

You will answer an expository writing prompt using sources and a rubric.

## ANALYZE THE RUBRIC

A rubric tells you what needs to be included in your writing.

**Purpose, Focus, and Organization**

Read the highlighted bullet. What is a central idea?

_____

_____

Read the third bullet. **Circle** the reason it is important to use transitional strategies.

**Evidence and Elaboration**

What is an elaborative technique that you have used in your writing?

_____

Read the last bullet. Rewrite these sentences to vary the sentence structure and end punctuation.
*The cat sits. The cat sees a mouse. The cat pounces.*

_____

# Expository Writing Rubric

### Purpose, Focus, and Organization • Score 4

- stays focused on the purpose, audience, and task
- **clearly presents and fully develops the central idea about a topic**
- uses transitional strategies, such as words and phrases, to connect ideas
- uses a logical text structure to organize information
- begins with a strong introduction and ends with a strong conclusion

### Evidence and Elaboration • Score 4

- effectively supports the central idea with convincing facts and details
- has strong examples of relevant evidence, or supporting details, from multiple sources
- uses elaborative techniques, such as facts, examples, definitions, and quotations from sources
- expresses interesting ideas clearly using precise language
- uses appropriate academic and domain-specific language
- uses different sentence structures

Turn to page 240 for the complete Expository Writing Rubric.

# Central Idea

**Stating the Central Idea** A strong expository essay has a clear central idea. All the details and facts are related to the central idea and help inform the reader about the topic.

**Task**

As you write your essay, consider what the task and purpose are. If you are presenting ideas on a topic, you will use formal language. If you are discussing ideas with a partner, you will use informal language.

> People have used coins as currency for a long time. China began using metal coins as a form of currency around 1000 B.C. The coins varied in shape, size, and worth. By the 7th century B.C., coins made of precious metals such as silver and gold became popular in Europe and the Middle East. I collect coins. After being weighed on a scale to determine their value, coins were stamped with designs that stated their worth.

Read the paragraph above. Underline the central idea. Write an example of a transitional phrase that introduces new facts about metal coins.

_____

_____

_____

**Details** Writers use relevant details as evidence to support and develop their central idea. These relevant, or supporting, details also help keep the essay focused on the central idea. Strong writers do not include unimportant details in their writing.

Reread the paragraph above. Cross out an unimportant detail that does NOT support the central idea.

## ANALYZE THE STUDENT MODEL

**Paragraphs 1–2**

The central idea is highlighted in paragraph 1 of John's essay. What is an example of relevant evidence in paragraph 2 that John uses to support his central idea?

_____

_____

_____

**Underline** the detail that tells you what incident first sparked Bath's interest in science.

**What source does John use to tell about how Bath was inspired at a young age?**

_____

_____

_____

**Circle** an example of elaboration that John uses in paragraph 2.

# Student Model: Expository Essay

John responded to the Writing Prompt: *Write an expository essay about Dr. Patricia Bath and her invention of the Laserphaco Probe.* Read John's essay below.

**1**   In many different ways, Dr. Patricia Bath spent much of her life helping people with visual impairments. Many people remember her for her invention of the Laserphaco Probe. This is a tool for removing cataracts, or cloudy eye lenses. However, Bath also cared a lot about helping everyone get eye care. She found new ways to make that possible.

**2**   Born in New York City's Harlem neighborhood in 1942, Bath lived with parents who encouraged her to dream big. At that time, the Bath family faced obstacles as African Americans. But Bath didn't let that discourage her. According to the article "Patricia Bath: The Early Years," Bath's mother gave her a chemistry set when she was little. This inspired Bath to dream of being a scientist. Her first scientific discovery happened when she was only 16. She found an equation related to cancer cell growth while at a summer science program. It was important enough to be included in a scientific paper. Bath went on to study ophthalmology, or eye care. According to the article "Eyes on the Prize," she was the first African American ophthalmology resident at New York University.

Titus Group/Shutterstock; Nata Studio/Shutterstock

3      Bath was concerned that African Americans were more likely to have visual impairments than white Americans. The problem was getting access to eye care. She came up with the idea of community ophthalmology, in which volunteers help give eye care. Bath also created the American Institute for the Prevention of Blindness.

4      Bath's most important invention helped remove cataracts. These are cloudy eye lenses that can lead to blindness. According to "The History of Cataract Surgery," people tried many things to fix cataracts. For many years, doctors tried pushing them out of place. This didn't work well and still led to blindness. Around 1750, doctors began to take them out through surgery. But Bath's invention, the Laserphaco Probe, dissolves the cloudy lens. This is much quicker and less painful than older methods. After the lens is dissolved, a doctor can replace it with an artificial one.

5      As a child, Bath loved pretending to be a scientist. As an adult, her ideas and inventions did a lot to help people with visual impairments. Bath's work should inspire people to never give up on their dreams.

**Paragraph 3**

What is an example of evidence that John provides to support the idea that Bath cared about helping other people?

_____

_____

_____

**Paragraph 4**

**Circle** a transitional phrase that John uses in paragraph 4.

**Paragraph 5**

In his last paragraph, how does John restate an idea introduced in the second paragraph and tie it to his central idea?

_____

_____

_____

## Apply the Rubric

With a partner, use the rubric on page 212 to discuss why John scored a 4 on his essay.

# WRITING

**My Goal** I can write an expository essay.

## Analyze the Prompt

### Writing Prompt

*Write an expository essay on the positive impacts of technology.*

**Purpose, Audience, and Task** Reread the writing prompt. What is your purpose for writing? My purpose is to ______________________

______________________________________________

Who will your audience be? My audience will be ______________

______________________________________________

What type of writing is the prompt asking for? ______________

______________________________________________

**Set a Purpose for Reading Sources** Asking questions about the positive impacts that technology has made will help you identify what you already know about the impacts of technology. Before you read the passages, write a question here.

______________________________________________

______________________________________________

______________________________________________

______________________________________________

New Africa/Shutterstock

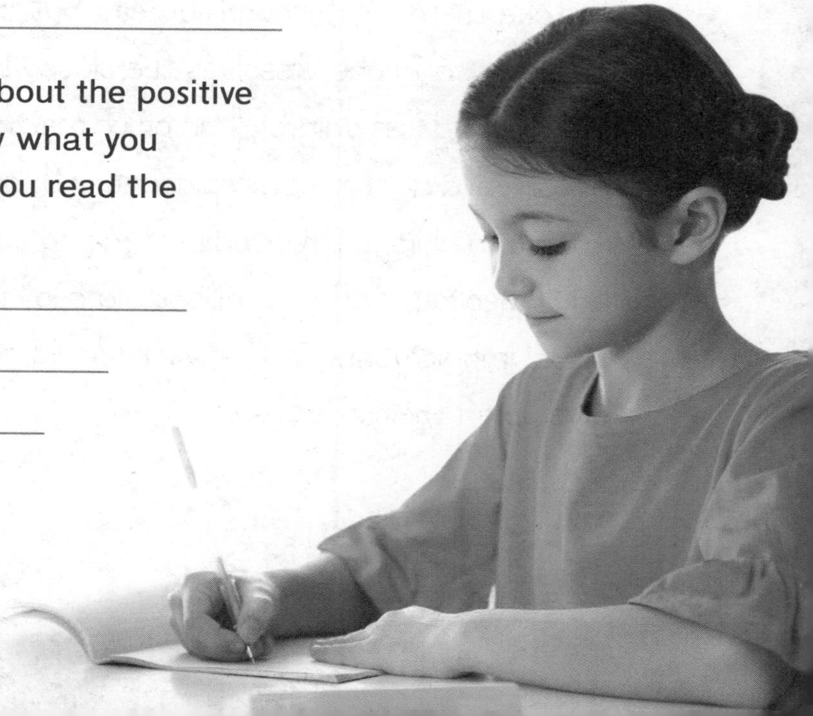

**SOURCE 1**

# How Technology Is Aiding Senior Citizens

1    The number of senior citizens, or older adults, will double by 2050. Like most people, senior citizens use technology for many reasons. **However, some senior citizens have special challenges. They can be aided by special kinds of technology.** Many technology companies are answering the call and making special devices for the senior citizen market.

2    An issue some older adults face is loneliness. Senior citizens may become isolated when they lose friends or family members. Illnesses might confine people to their homes for long periods of time. Technology companies are creating robot companions to help. Some robots have artificial intelligence. They can start conversations, answer questions, and remind senior citizens to take medicines. Other robots are interactive pets. The popularity of these robots proves that you are never too old to play!

3    Some senior citizens require special medical treatments and therapies. Some older adults have a disease or injury that affects their brains. They often require therapy to help their brains recover. One company has created a virtual reality headset. It makes therapy more like a game. The headset also records how the patient is doing. It can then recommend changes to the therapy based on that data.

4    Thousands of companies are working to create new technological devices for senior citizens. Their new inventions will help older adults live happier and healthier lives.

julos/iStock/Getty Images

## EXPOSITORY ESSAY

### FIND TEXT EVIDENCE

**Paragraph 1**
**Underline** the detail that tells you how technology companies are helping senior citizens.

**Paragraph 2**
The central idea in paragraph 1 is highlighted. **Circle** the central idea in paragraph 2.

How can robots help some senior citizens?

_____

_____

_____

**Paragraph 3**
**Draw a box** around the details describing how a virtual reality headset helps with brain therapy.

**Paragraph 4**
How will new technologies and inventions help senior citizens?

_____

_____

**Take Notes** Paraphrase the central idea of the source and give examples of details that support this idea.

## FIND TEXT EVIDENCE 🔍

**Paragraphs 5–6**

The central idea in paragraph 5 has been highlighted for you. **Underline** supporting details in paragraph 6. What is the difference between orthotics and prosthetics?

_____

_____

_____

**Paragraph 7**

**Circle** the detail that tells you what invention helped to make changes to prosthetic designs easier.

**Paragraph 8**

What fact about advancing technology will help animals?

_____

_____

_____

**Take Notes** Paraphrase the central idea of the source and give examples of details that support that idea.

SOURCE
2

# The New Science of Animal Prosthetics

5     Meet Mosha, a very special elephant. Mosha is the first elephant to ever receive a working prosthetic leg! When Mosha was seven months old, she lost a leg in an accident. Mosha was lucky. An elephant hospital in Thailand accepted her. A doctor who helps people in need of artificial limbs heard about Mosha. He decided to try to create an artificial limb for her. It worked! **Animal prosthetics is now a growing and special technology.**

6     While orthotics correct the use of a body part, prosthetics replace a body part with an artificial part. Before the 2000s, such devices for animals were rare. Then, in 2005, one pioneer made an artificial leg for a Labrador retriever. It was a success! Now, special companies focus entirely on animal prosthetics and orthotics. Although dogs are the most common recipients, one company has aided other animals as well, including bald eagles, goats, sheep, turtles, and a gazelle.

7     It takes special knowledge and skill to properly create devices to help different animals. Specialists must study an animal's movements. Then, they create a plaster cast that is used to design a plastic and metal limb. Using a 3D printer makes changing the design much easier. Instead of making a new plaster cast, a designer can resize the design file on a computer and print a new prosthetic limb!

8     As technology related to prosthetics advances, the costs are going down. For animals like Mosha, that's a good thing. More affordable prosthetics can allow more animals with disabilities to live longer, happier lives.

# HEALTHCARE AND DRONES

9    In 2018, the US territory of Puerto Rico was hit hard by Hurricane Maria. An aid organization decided to test a faster way of sending help. It used drones to send emergency medical supplies. A drone is a type of aircraft with no onboard pilot. It is controlled either by a person using equipment remotely or by an onboard computer. The organization's drones flew over destroyed roads to mountain villages. They dropped off needed supplies. The test was a success!

10   Before the early 2000s, it was mostly the military who used drones. However, in the 2010s, technology companies started working on developing non-military drones. They developed drones that could make deliveries.

11   Today, drones do a lot of important work in the field of medical care. In some countries, drones deliver tests directly from patients to remote laboratories. In others, they bring vaccines to clinics. In the fall of 2020, during the COVID-19 pandemic, a large drug company in North Carolina tested temperature-controlled vaccine delivery using drones.

12   Some people have concerns about drones. They wonder if drones could be used to invade people's privacy. Others worry about drone accidents. The Federal Aviation Administration continues to develop drone rules. In 2020, for example, the FAA said drones must have remote IDs. This lets officials know where drones are and who controls them. With the right safeguards in place, drones can be a good way of getting supplies to people in need.

## FIND TEXT EVIDENCE 🔍

**Paragraph 9**
**Circle** the detail that tells how an organization helped Puerto Rico after Hurricane Maria. How did this organization help?

_____

_____

**Paragraphs 10–11**
**Underline** the detail that tells how drone use changed in the 2010s.

In what field are drones doing important work today?

_____

_____

**Paragraphs 12**
**Draw a box** around details that show areas where people are concerned about drones.

**Circle** text that shows how the FAA is answering safety concerns.

📝 **Take Notes** Paraphrase the central idea of the source and give examples of details that support this idea.

Mopic/Shutterstock

**My Goal** I can synthesize information from three sources.

## TAKE NOTES

Read the writing prompt below. Then use the three sources, your notes, and the graphic organizer to plan a response.

**Writing Prompt** *Write an expository essay on the positive impacts of technology.*

_____

_____

### Synthesize Information

Review your notes and annotations from each source. Think about these technological advances. What do they have in common? Discuss your ideas with your partner.

## Plan: Organize Ideas

**Introduction**

State the Central Idea

Modern technology is . . .

**Body**

Supporting Idea

Technology can help . . .

Supporting Idea

Supporting Idea

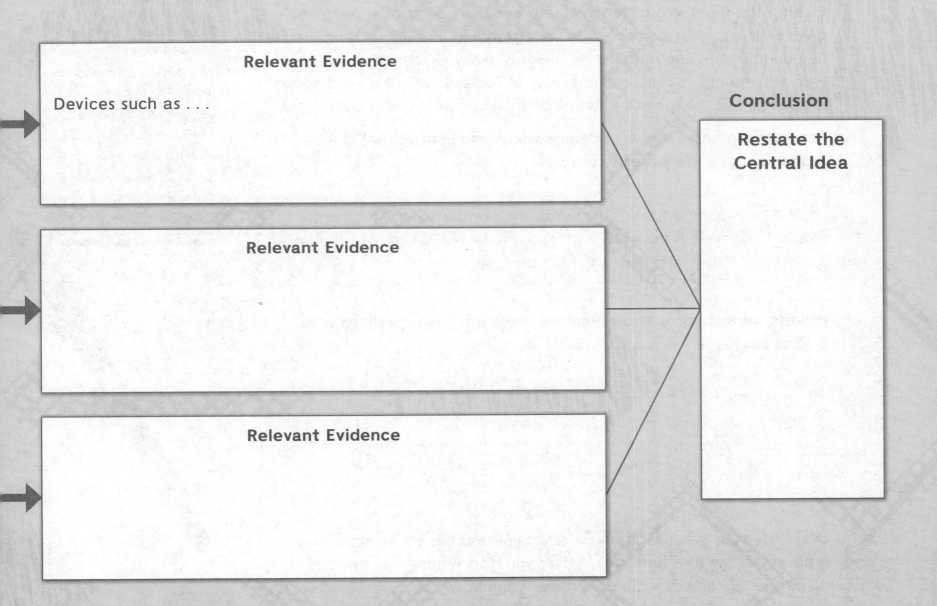

**Relevant Evidence**

Devices such as . . .

**Relevant Evidence**

**Relevant Evidence**

**Conclusion**

**Restate the Central Idea**

# Draft: Precise Language

**Picking the Right Word** Writers use precise, or specific, language to give readers a clear and accurate understanding of a topic. Using precise language means choosing the right words to say exactly what you mean. Precise language is concrete, not general. For example, the word *animal* is general, but the specific noun *elephant* is concrete and precise.

Read the sentences below. Underline words and phrases that can be replaced with a more precise word.

> What I love about Miami is the sandy areas by the water. My favorite thing to do is go in the water and move my arms and legs, which moves me through the water. The water is a nice color.

Rewrite the sentences above. Replace the words you underlined with precise language.

_____

_____

_____

_____

_____

**Draft** Use your graphic organizer and the examples above to write your draft in your writer's notebook. Before you start writing, review the rubric on page 212. Remember to use precise language.

### Grammar Connections

Use a comma before a conjunction that joins independent clauses in a compound sentence:

*I like the lake, and my mom likes the pool.*

between a city and a state:

*Detroit, Michigan*

between the day and year in a date:

*March 3, 1845*

CHECK IN   1   2   3   4

# Revise: Peer Conferences

**Review a Draft** Listen actively to your partner. Take notes about what you liked and what was difficult to follow. Begin by telling what you liked. Use these sentence starters:

*I like the evidence you used to support the central idea because . . .*
*What did you mean by . . .*
*I think adding precise language will help to . . .*

After you give each other feedback, reflect on the peer conference. How can you use the guidance from your partner to help improve your writing?

_____

_____

_____

**Revision** Use the Revising Checklist to help you figure out what text you may need to move, elaborate on, or delete. After you finish writing your final draft, use the full rubric on pages 240–243 to score your essay.

### Revising Checklist

- [ ] Does my writing have a strong central idea?
- [ ] Did I include enough relevant evidence to support my central idea?
- [ ] Did I use good transitional strategies to show the connections between ideas?
- [ ] Did I use precise language?
- [ ] Did I check my spelling and punctuation?

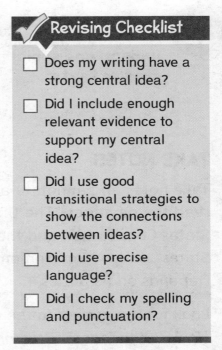

Turn to page 199. Fill in the bars to show what you learned.

| My Score | | | |
|---|---|---|---|
| Purpose, Focus, & Organization (4 pts) | Evidence & Elaboration (4 pts) | Conventions (2 pts) | Total (10 pts) |
| | | | |

**I can read and understand social studies texts.**

## TAKE NOTES

Take notes and annotate as you read the passages "The United States Constitution and the Rights of States" and "A Government That Depends on Its States."

Look for the answer to the question: *How do the federal government and state governments compare?*

_____

_____

_____

_____

_____

_____

_____

_____

**PASSAGE 1**

EXPOSITORY TEXT

# The United States Constitution and the Rights of States

What is an amendment to the constitution? An amendment modifies, or changes, the constitution. A Congressional majority can amend the constitution. In 1787, the 10th Amendment was adopted. It addressed the amount of power the newly formed government would have. The founding fathers did not want to see the United States follow in the path of Britain. They didn't want an all-powerful government over the people. The 10th Amendment was proposed to protect people's rights. This amendment says that powers not given to the federal government in the Constitution belong to the states and the people. The founding fathers believed that this was the path to liberty. By bringing government power closer to home, the people would have the opportunity for liberty and freedoms that do not exist under a strong, centralized government.

The state constitutions resemble the US Constitution. Like the US Constitution, state constitutions establish a three-branch structure of government. Each state constitution also has its own Bill of Rights. State constitutions also differ from the US Constitution. State constitutions usually include specifics that only affect the people of that state. The rules for amending a state constitution are different from that of the federal constitution. It is less complicated to propose and pass amendments at the state level. For example, a petition by citizens can lead to an amendment proposal.

Even though each state has its own constitution, the federal government is still considered the "supreme law of the land," and each

stoyarom/E+/Getty Images

state must follow the laws of the US Constitution. This fact became critical in the aftermath of the Civil War. Following the Civil War, several amendments were passed in order to establish and protect the rights of all US citizens.

**PASSAGE 2** EXPOSITORY TEXT

# A Government That Depends on Its States

Why does the federal government depend on its states? The Constitution gives the federal government a limited list of powers and responsibilities. All other responsibilities belong to the states. This means that the federal government must rely on the states in order to fully meet the needs of citizens.

The chart below shows some of the different duties of the federal and state governments.

| Duties of Government | |
|---|---|
| **Federal Government** | **State Governments** |
| • Writes Laws | • Establish Local Governments |
| • Prints Money | • Issue Licenses (Driving, Marriage, etc.) |
| • Supports Post Offices and Makes Postage Stamps | • Hold Elections |
| • Regulates International and Interstate Commerce | • Regulate State Commerce |
| • Develops and Supports the Military Branches | • Provide for Public Health and Safety |
| • Signs Treaties and Declares War | • Establish Public Schools |

## TAKE NOTES

_____

_____

_____

_____

_____

_____

_____

_____

_____

_____

_____

_____

_____

_____

_____

_____

_____

_____

_____

States are responsible for many of the services that citizens rely on in their everyday lives, such as schools, hospitals, police and fire departments, and public transportation. They are also in charge of building and maintaining roads, creating state parks, and setting rules for businesses within the state.

State governments have many responsibilities, so they often grant some of their powers to local governments. Local governments can then pass laws or provide services in the way that works best for each community.

The federal government is limited in how much power it has over the states. However, the federal government can negotiate with a state to change its rules. For example, the federal government may offer a state extra money for building roads if it agrees to lower the speed limit.

The federal government must depend on the states to carry out many government duties. Citizens rely on these state duties. By working together, the federal and state governments can use their specific powers to serve and protect citizens and create a better country for everyone.

## COMPARE THE PASSAGES

Review your notes from both passages. Then create a Venn diagram like the one below. Use your notes and the diagram to record how the information in the two passages is alike and different.

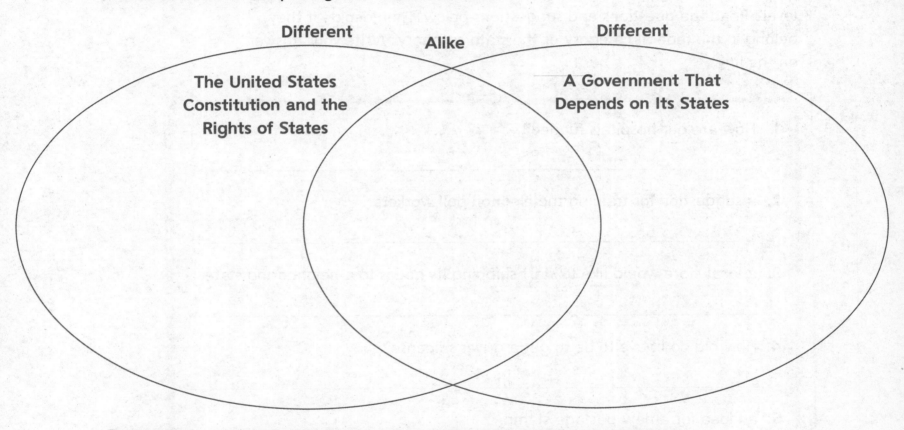

**Different**

**Alike**

**Different**

The United States Constitution and the Rights of States

A Government That Depends on Its States

### Synthesize Information

Think about what you learned from the texts. How do the federal government and the state governments protect people's rights? How do the federal government and the state governments provide services for people? Write your ideas in your reader's notebook.

## FEDERAL OR STATE?

People within your state and community have questions about public services. They also have some suggestions for improvements. Are these questions and suggestions for someone at the federal level or the state level? Read the questions and suggestions below. Then decide if they belong in the federal category or the state category. Write your answer on the lines.

1. How are our hospitals funded?

   _____

2. a suggestion for training the election poll workers

   _____

3. a local store would like to start shipping its goods to a neighboring state

   _____

4. How old do I have to be to get a driver's license?

   _____

5. an idea for a new postage stamp

   _____

6. an idea for organizing clean-up days at the nature parks and wetland areas

   _____

## RESEARCH FACTS

Write down three facts from the table that you want to know more about. Research the three facts. Then write an article (it can be digital) using the facts. Add photographs or drawings to your article.

FACT 1: _____

_____

_____

FACT 2: _____

_____

_____

FACT 3: _____

_____

_____

_____

# CONNECT TO CONTENT

My Goal · I can read and understand science texts.

## TAKE NOTES

Take notes and annotate as you read the passages "Turn Up the Heat" and "3 . . . 2 . . . 1: We Have Spin-Off!"

Look for the answer to the question: *How has science improved our daily lives?*

_____

_____

_____

_____

_____

_____

_____

_____

_____

_____

_____

_____

# Turn Up the Heat

Thermal energy from the sun and our bodies keeps us warm. Thermal energy comes from the energy of moving particles of matter. The faster the particles move, the greater the amount of thermal energy. Heat is the flow of thermal energy from one object to another, and it always moves from warmer objects to cooler objects. One example of heat energy is when food is being cooked on a hot stove top. Heating can change the temperature of an object. Temperature measures the thermal energy of the particles in a substance.

Heat transfer takes place through conduction, convection, and radiation. Every day you probably see heat transfers take place without even realizing it. Solids are mostly heated by conduction. Conduction occurs within an object or when two objects are touching one another. Convection transfers heat through liquids or gases. Radiation travels through space—it doesn't need matter to transfer heat. The Sun's energy is transferred through space by radiation.

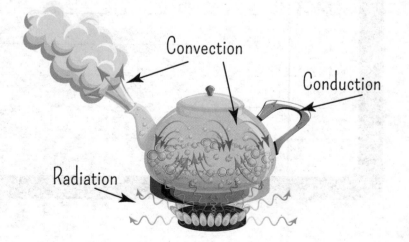

Conductors are materials that transfer heat. Some conductors transfer heat better than others. For example, many metals, such as silver, copper, aluminum, brass, iron, lead, and mercury, are good conductors. Things made from glass, wood, water, cork, cotton, and wool are bad conductors of heat.

Scientists use what they know about how heat transfers to develop new technologies. Use what you know to identify things that use conduction, convection, and radiation to transfer heat.

**PASSAGE 2** **EXPOSITORY TEXT**

# 3 . . . 2 . . . 1: We Have Spin-Off!

The technology created for the space program has led to many new products that have improved people's lives and businesses. These improvements and inventions are called spin-offs from the space program.

Many spin-offs can be found in homes and in grocery stores. Smoke detectors were developed decades ago for use on Skylab, America's first space station. Many stores carry freeze-dried foods in sealed packages. These foods were first developed for astronauts, who needed lightweight foods that would not spoil.

Spin-offs have also changed sports for athletes. Lightweight athletic shoes use padding and air-cushion soles that were first used in spacesuits. Many athletes use heart-rate monitors when they work out that were originally developed to keep track of an astronaut's health during long flights.

**TAKE NOTES**

## TAKE NOTES

_____
_____
_____
_____
_____
_____
_____
_____
_____
_____
_____
_____
_____
_____
_____
_____
_____
_____
_____

Spin-offs do more than make life easier; they keep people safe as well. Improvements in video cameras used in space now help protect people. Face masks, breathing systems, and fire suits used by firefighters today were developed from spacesuits worn by astronauts.

Spin-offs are also helping people with diseases and disabilities. Today, doctors can take clear images of human organs with scanning equipment. These specialized cameras are spin-offs from space program research. Space program research on robotics has led to breakthroughs in artificial limbs.

These are only some of the spin-offs in our daily lives. There simply isn't enough "space" to list them all here. Look around you. What other spin-offs can you discover?

(tr) James A. McDivitt/The LIFE Picture Collection/Getty Images; (bl to r) D. Hurst/Alamy Stock Photo, Stockdisc/Getty Images, John B. Carnett/Popular Science/Getty Images

## COMPARE THE PASSAGES

Review your notes from both passages. Then create a Venn diagram like the one below. Use your notes and the diagram to record how the information in the two passages is alike and different.

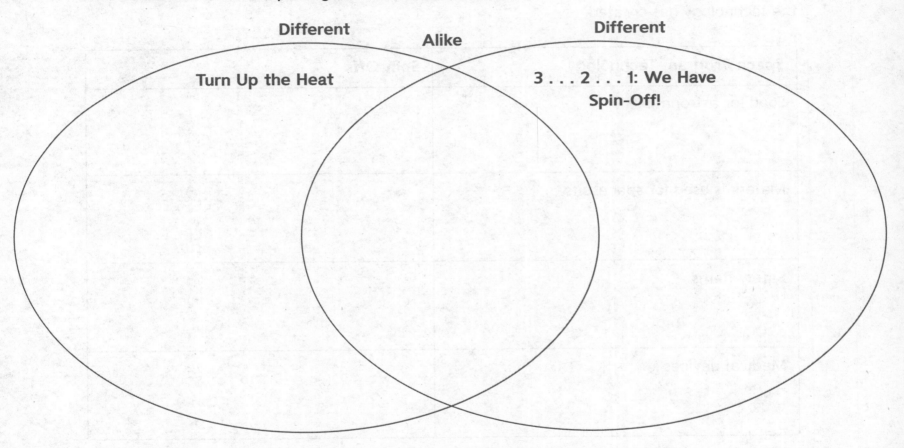

**Different**  **Alike**  **Different**

**Turn Up the Heat**  **3 . . . 2 . . . 1: We Have Spin-Off!**

### Synthesize Information

Think about what you learned from the texts. What technologies mentioned in the texts do you use in your everyday life? Write your ideas in your reader's notebook.

CHECK IN  1  2  3  4

## SPACE TO EARTH

Reread "3 . . . 2 . . . 1: We Have Spin-Off!" and think about the ways space program technologies have improved life on Earth. Complete the chart below with the spin-offs that were created from the space program. Then research other items the technology has created.

| Space Program Technology | Spin-Offs |
|---|---|
| Food for astronauts | |
| Materials used for spacesuits | |
| Safety items | |
| Medical devices | |

# Reflect on Your Learning

**Talk About It** Reflect on what you learned in this unit. Then talk with a partner about how you did.

I am really proud of how I can _____

_____

_____

_____

Something I need to work more on is _____

_____

_____

_____

_____

**My Goal** Set a goal for Unit 5. In your reader's notebook, write about what you can do to get there.

Share a goal you have with a partner.

# Argumentative Writing Rubric

| Score | Purpose, Focus, and Organization (4-point Rubric) | Evidence and Elaboration (4-point Rubric) | Conventions of Standard English (2-point Rubric begins at score point 2) |
|---|---|---|---|
| 4 | • stays focused on the purpose, audience, and task<br>• makes a claim that clearly supports a perspective<br>• uses transitional strategies, such as words and phrases, to connect ideas<br>• presents ideas in a logical progression, or order<br>• begins with a strong introduction and ends with a strong conclusion | • effectively supports the claim with logical reasons<br>• has strong examples of relevant evidence, or supporting details, from multiple sources<br>• uses elaborative techniques, such as examples, definitions, and quotations from sources<br>• expresses interesting ideas clearly using precise language<br>• uses appropriate academic and domain-specific language<br>• uses different sentence structures | |

| Score | Purpose, Focus, and Organization (4-point Rubric) | Evidence and Elaboration (4-point Rubric) | Conventions of Standard English (2-point Rubric begins at score point 2) |
|---|---|---|---|
| 3 | • generally stays focused on the purpose, audience, and task<br>• makes a claim that mostly supports a perspective<br>• uses some transitional strategies, such as words and phrases, to connect ideas<br>• presents ideas in a mostly logical progression, or order<br>• begins with an acceptable introduction and ends with a sufficient conclusion | • mostly supports the claim with some logical reasons<br>• has some examples of mostly relevant evidence, or supporting details, from multiple sources<br>• uses some elaborative techniques, such as examples, definitions, and quotations from sources<br>• generally expresses interesting ideas using both precise and general language<br>• mostly uses appropriate academic and domain-specific language<br>• mostly uses different sentence structures | |

# Argumentative Writing Rubric

| Score | Purpose, Focus, and Organization (4-point Rubric) | Evidence and Elaboration (4-point Rubric) | Conventions of Standard English (2-point Rubric) |
|---|---|---|---|
| 2 | • stays somewhat focused on the purpose, audience, and task, but may include unimportant details<br><br>• does not make a clear claim or does not completely support a perspective<br><br>• uses few transitional strategies to connect ideas<br><br>• may present ideas that do not follow a logical progression, or order<br><br>• may begin with an inadequate introduction or end with an unsatisfactory conclusion | • shows some support of the claim with logical reasons<br><br>• has weak and inappropriate examples of evidence or does not include enough sources<br><br>• may not use elaborative techniques effectively<br><br>• expresses some interesting ideas, but ideas are simple and vague<br><br>• uses limited academic and domain-specific language<br><br>• may use only simple sentence structures | • has a sufficient command of grammar and usage<br><br>• has a sufficient command of capitalization, punctuation, spelling, and sentence formation<br><br>• has slight errors in grammar and usage that do not affect meaning |

| Score | Purpose, Focus, and Organization (4-point Rubric) | Evidence and Elaboration (4-point Rubric) | Conventions of Standard English (2-point Rubric) |
|---|---|---|---|
| 1 | • is not aware of the purpose, audience, and task<br>• does not make a claim or does not support a perspective<br>• uses few or no transitional strategies to connect ideas<br>• does not present ideas in a logical progression, or order<br>• does not include an introduction nor a conclusion | • supports the claim with few logical reasons or does not support the claim at all<br>• has few or no examples of evidence or does not include enough sources<br>• does not use elaborative techniques<br>• has confusing or unclear ideas or does not express any interesting ideas<br>• does not demonstrate a grasp of academic and domain-specific language<br>• consists only of simple sentence structures | • has an incomplete command of grammar and usage<br>• has an incomplete command of capitalization, punctuation, spelling, and sentence formation<br>• has some errors in grammar and usage that may affect meaning |
| 0 | | | • does not have a command of grammar and usage<br>• does not have a command of capitalization, punctuation, spelling, and sentence formation<br>• has too many serious errors in grammar and usage that frequently disrupt meaning |

# Expository Writing Rubric

| Score | Purpose, Focus, and Organization (4-point Rubric) | Evidence and Elaboration (4-point Rubric) | Conventions of Standard English (2-point Rubric begins at score point 2) |
|---|---|---|---|
| 4 | • stays focused on the purpose, audience, and task<br>• clearly presents and fully develops the central idea about a topic<br>• uses transitional strategies, such as words and phrases, to connect ideas<br>• uses a logical text structure to organize information<br>• begins with a strong introduction and ends with a strong conclusion | • effectively supports the central idea with convincing facts and details<br>• has strong examples of relevant evidence, or supporting details, from multiple sources<br>• uses elaborative techniques, such as facts, examples, definitions, and quotations from sources<br>• expresses interesting ideas clearly using precise language<br>• uses appropriate academic and domain-specific language<br>• uses different sentence structures | |

| Score | Purpose, Focus, and Organization (4-point Rubric) | Evidence and Elaboration (4-point Rubric) | Conventions of Standard English (2-point Rubric begins at score point 2) |
|---|---|---|---|
| 3 | • generally stays focused on the purpose, audience, and task<br>• presents and develops the central idea about a topic in a mostly clear and complete way, although there may be some unimportant details<br>• uses some transitional strategies, such as words and phrases, to connect ideas<br>• uses a mostly logical text structure to organize information<br>• begins with an acceptable introduction and ends with a sufficient conclusion | • mostly supports the central idea with some convincing facts and details<br>• has some examples of mostly relevant evidence, or supporting details, from multiple sources<br>• uses some elaborative techniques, such as facts, examples, definitions, and quotations from sources<br>• generally expresses interesting ideas using both precise and general language<br>• mostly uses appropriate academic and domain-specific language<br>• mostly uses different sentence structures | |

# Expository Writing Rubric

| Score | Purpose, Focus, and Organization (4-point Rubric) | Evidence and Elaboration (4-point Rubric) | Conventions of Standard English (2-point Rubric) |
|---|---|---|---|
| 2 | • stays somewhat focused on the purpose, audience, and task, but may include unimportant details<br><br>• does not clearly present or develop a central idea<br><br>• uses few transitional strategies to connect ideas<br><br>• may not follow a logical text structure to organize information<br><br>• may begin with an inadequate introduction or end with an unsatisfactory conclusion | • shows some support of the central idea with few convincing facts and details<br><br>• has weak and inappropriate examples of evidence or does not include enough sources<br><br>• may not use elaborative techniques effectively<br><br>• expresses some interesting ideas, but ideas are simple and vague<br><br>• uses limited academic and domain-specific language<br><br>• may use only simple sentence structures | • has a sufficient command of grammar and usage<br><br>• has a sufficient command of capitalization, punctuation, spelling, and sentence formation<br><br>• has slight errors in grammar and usage that do not affect meaning |

| Score | Purpose, Focus, and Organization (4-point Rubric) | Evidence and Elaboration (4-point Rubric) | Conventions of Standard English (2-point Rubric) |
|---|---|---|---|
| 1 | • is not aware of the purpose, audience, and task<br>• does not have a central idea<br>• uses few or no transitional strategies to connect ideas<br>• does not follow a logical text structure to organize information<br>• does not include an introduction nor a conclusion | • supports the central idea with few facts and details or does not support the central idea at all<br>• has few or no examples of evidence or does not include enough sources<br>• does not use elaborative techniques<br>• has confusing or unclear ideas or does not express any interesting ideas<br>• does not demonstrate a grasp of academic and domain-specific language<br>• consists only of simple sentence structures | • has an incomplete command of grammar and usage<br>• has an incomplete command of capitalization, punctuation, spelling, and sentence formation<br>• has some errors in grammar and usage that may affect meaning |
| 0 | | | • does not have a command of grammar and usage<br>• does not have a command of capitalization, punctuation, spelling, and sentence formation<br>• has too many serious errors in grammar and usage that frequently disrupt meaning |